MY VOCATION IS LOVE

Jean Lafrance

MY VOCATION IS LOVE
Thérèse of Lisieux

sp

St Paul Publications

MY VOCATION IS LOVE

Original title
MA VOCATION C'EST L'AMOUR
© Mediaspaul, 8 rue Madame, 75006 PARIS

English translation by Sr Anne Marie Brennan OCD

English edition
© St Paul Publications, Homebush, 1990

Australian edition
First published, November 1990

Cover design & photo: Bruno Colombari SSP

National Library of Australia
Card Number and ISBN 0 949080 84 5

Published by
ST PAUL PUBLICATIONS — Society of St Paul,
60-70 Broughton Road — Homebush, NSW 2140

Typeset and printed by Society of St Paul, Wantirna South, Victoria

St Paul Publications is an activity of the Priests and Brothers of the Society of St Paul who proclaim the Gospel through the media of social communication

Contents

Abbreviations

Ms A, B, C   The three autobiographical manuscripts of St Thérèse, published under the title, _Story of a Soul._

LC   Last conversations of St Thérèse with her sisters, Mother Agnès of Jesus, Sr Marie of the Sacred Heart, Sr Geneviève.

LT   Letters of St Thérèse.

CSG   _Counsels and Reminiscences_, published by Sr Geneviève, 1952. English translation, _A Memoir of my Sister, St Thérèse._

Introduction

'To me, he has given his infinite mercy'

If Jesus Christ rose from the dead and is alive, he must be living somewhere and we must be able to find his address so that we can meet him and make contact with him; otherwise to affirm Jesus' resurrection is to set up a dispute turning merely on verbal points. Of course, there are special places where we can meet him and I am thinking in particular of the Eucharist and the Gospel. But I wonder if I would give these two addresses at once to someone who asks me and expresses the desire to 'see' Christ. Reading the Gospel is not the first thing to do, but it is by no means the last!

I believe that if Jesus is living today he can be met in those men and women we call the saints, who can say with St Paul: *It is no longer I who live, it is Christ living in me* (Gal 2:20). So firstly these are the people to meet, see them living, and only after that, read the Gospel to understand what makes 'that person' tick, what makes a saint, that is one in whom the risen Christ is living.

If Thérèse of Lisieux were still living, I would advise all who wish to meet such a saint to go and see her now and then. Her life does not belong to prehistory: a few years ago (1959), one of her sisters, Céline, was alive and she had known her well since she had been her novice. But you have to be very attentive and, as Fr Molinié says, 'be sharp-eyed' otherwise you can pass by a saint without realising it. This is what happened with Thérèse: most of the sisters who lived with her did not suspect that they were living with a saint, perhaps the greatest of modern times, and one of them even wondered what good could be written about her after her death. This is why we do not have to wait for saints to be canonised before meeting them. There is a crowd of anonymous and 'non-commissioned' saints, who are living out in the world as well as in convents, but they are well hidden and hide themselves so that their beauty is known to God alone. And I can assure you that if the Holy Spirit is living in you, he will give you 'the eye' to see and meet them. You will have no trouble tracking them down, for 'they look like Jesus Christ' and like him they are gentle and humble.

Now, if you want a specific and easy-to-find address, I can give you one: that of Thérèse of the Child Jesus. Call her, pray to her, ask her for a grace or tell her that you would like to meet her. It does not matter how you approach her — there may be just something that is not going along so well in your life — the important thing is to get in touch with her. As a priest, I can say that you never pray to her in vain, very quickly you feel her presence, especially if your prayer is humble, confident and persevering.

Her presence and her mission

You will not perhaps see her physically, as some soldiers had the privilege of seeing her at the front, but I can guarantee that those who begin to discover Thérèse's presence in their lives and in their hearts will not be prevented from loving her, praying to her and sensing her spiritual presence: she had only one great desire, to see Jesus living in her, and that very desire intensifies love. And I say this not only because of the experience of those who pray to her, but also because of the conviction Thérèse herself had before she died. She was

8

very quickly convinced that 'her premature death would not mark the beginning of an early retirement' (Fr Descouvemont, *Sur les pas de Thérèse*, 230). She knew that she would come back to earth for she was not dying, but entering into life.

She wrote to Fr Roulland, a missionary in China: *If I am going to heaven soon, I will ask Jesus' permission to visit you in Su-Tchuen, and we will continue our apostolate together* (30 July, 1896, LT 193). And on 24 February 1897, she wrote to Abbé Bellière, her other spiritual brother: *I do not know the future. However, if Jesus grants my presentiments, I promise that I will still be your little sister in heaven. Our union, far from being broken, will become deeper. Then there will be no more enclosure, no more grilles and my soul will be able to fly with you to the distant missions* (LT 220).

Furthermore, she was very keenly aware of her posthumous mission; not only was she certain that she would come back to earth, but she felt that she would spend her heaven making Love loved. During the night of 16-17 July 1897, at two o'clock in the morning, after another haemoptysis, she said:

> *I feel that I am about to enter into my rest ... But I also feel that my mission is going to begin, my mission to make God loved as I love him, to give my little way to souls. If God grants my desires, my heaven will be spent on earth, until the end of time. Yes, I want to spend my heaven doing good on earth. This is not impossible, since from the very heart of the beatific vision, the Angels watch over us* (LC 17.7).

She went even further in her presentiment of her mission since she was also convinced that she would answer those who would pray to her by allowing them to experience the power of her intercession with the Father. Some time before she died a life of St Louis de Gonzague was read in the refectory of the Carmel which told how he had cured a dying priest by strewing a shower of roses on his bed. Coming out of the refectory, Thérèse had leaned on a piece of furniture and said to Sr Marie of the Sacred Heart: *And I too, after my death, will let fall a shower of roses* (LC 9.6).

Such a statement borders on the absurd, or it could be taken as delirium. This was not the case with Thérèse who had her feet firmly planted on the ground. She knew that God is all-powerful and that nothing is impossible for him. Besides, having refused him nothing on earth, Thérèse was sure that God would refuse her nothing in heaven. This is why everyone would love her. On 14 September, when she had just unpetalled some roses over her crucifix and these petals were falling from her bed onto the infirmary floor, Thérèse added very seriously: *Gather up these petals carefully, my little sisters, they will help you perform favours later. Do not lose any of them* (LC 14.9).

'To make you loved' (Act of Offering)

And now, if someone asks what is this mission of Thérèse I will reply with the very words of her act of Offering: *O my God! Blessed Trinity, I desire to love you and to make you loved* (cf. Clarke, p. 276). As we have said above, she herself described that mission: *To make God loved*. You could say that Thérèse's passionate desire had been 'to make Love loved', if you are not afraid of paraphrasing St Augustine: 'I loved Love before loving what it was' (*Conf.* 111, 1,1). On 9 June 1895, *I was given the grace to understand more than ever before how much Jesus wants to be loved* (Ms A 180). Thérèse believed in love and surrendered herself to it with absolute confidence.

But it was not just a question of any love. *To me, she said, he has given his infinite mercy, and in its light I contemplate and adore the other divine perfections! ... Then everything seems to me resplendent with love, even Justice (and perhaps this even more than all the others) seems to me clothed in love* (Ms A 180). For Thérèse, love is above all mercy, that is, the foolish love of the Father who looks for his prodigal child because it is wounded, sick and even a sinner.

Usually when we speak about love, we conjure up firstly the human attitude: *If I were to give away all that I have to the hungry, if I give over my body to be burned,* and St Paul hastens to add: *if I do not have love, it would serve no purpose* (1 Cor 13:3). We therefore must have, receive and welcome love and not only give it. Thérèse understood perfectly that *love does not mean our love for God* (1 Jn 4:10). This is surely the most important line in the New Testament which explains the love of the Trinity and the Incarnation of the Word.

If this is not too trite, says Fr Molinié again: 'Love consists in that we do not love'. As long as we have not grasped this by experiencing our own incapacity to love, as long as we are not at home with this word in our hearts, then charity will not be at home in our hearts and it will not flow in us: it will struggle in the midst of numerous agitations.

We have first of all to experience that we do not love, that we are incapable of breaking the circle which closes us in on ourselves and accept this fact, allowing ourselves to be completely convinced by it. Otherwise charity will remain for us just a good desire, a sterile germ incapable of producing genuine fruit.

Fortunately there is a sequence to St John's words: *He has loved us first and has given us his Son for the expiation of our sins* (1 Jn 4:10). To be consoled by the second part of the sentence, we have to have swallowed the first: but I admit that to swallow the first, we need to have been helped by the second! We then begin to love God and our neighbour with a love which is an infinitely poor, wavering and insufficient response to the infinite Love surrounding our hearts of stone' (Molinié, *Adoration ou Désespoir*, 282).

This was Thérèse's secret in her discovery of merciful Love. We still stand in wonder at the summit of love that she attained, but we can scarcely guess at the depths of nothingness into which she descended in order to be raised to this height of love. She lived out what St John of the Cross says: 'I went down so low, so low ... so that I could be lifted up so high, so high'.[1]

In her letter to her godmother, Sr Marie of the Sacred Heart, she describes clearly this gymnastic which consists in a rebound from the depths of her own nothingness to the heights of merciful Love: *My dearest Godmother ... if all weak and imperfect souls felt what the smallest of souls feels, that is, the soul of your little Thérèse, no one would despair of reaching the summit of the mountain of Love, since Jesus does not ask for great deeds, but only abandonment and gratitude* (Ms B 188).

Some days we will be tempted to say: 'Ah, if I had but a fraction of Thérèse's will, I could achieve the same acts of love'! And Thérèse would answer us as she did her sisters who admired her heroic patience during her last illness: *Oh, it's not that!* Thérèse knew only too well that she was as weak as we are and as poor as her sisters, but she possessed a strength which did not come from herself and which was the very power of the Resurrection, or the power of merciful Love (which comes from the same source and which comes from the power of the Holy Spirit), poured forth in our hearts by the Spirit of Jesus. She could have said with St Michael

1 Thérèse herself quoted this text from *The Spiritual Canticle* in her letter to Sr Marie of the Sacred Heart. 'So, plunging down so low, so low into the depths of my own nothingness, I lifted myself so high, so high' that I attained my goal!' (Ms B, 195).

Garicoïts who was reproached for falling into ecstasy: 'How could I do otherwise?'

'A giant's course'

Thérèse understood in a wonderful way that God can only apply the remedy of love to those who know they are sick. Because she had plumbed the depths of her own powerlessness she was able to receive the Saviour's healing. Those who wish to love without knowing the humiliation of being poor and in need of love would be bitterly deceived, because they would think that they were loving and performing deeds of love, when they are under an illusion and unable to do so, because they are incapable of it.

To illustrate our point we must draw from Thérèse's life some 'miracles' − it is the word she herself uses (Ms A 97, 109) which brought about the successive healing of her wounds. All the pain caused by her mother's death vanished in 'the Virgin's ravishing smile'. She experienced real healing at that moment. But there still remained other wounds which kept her in 'the swaddling bands of infancy' and made her cry over trifles.

> *God would have to work a small miracle to make me grow up in an instant, and this miracle he performed on that unforgettable Christmas day (1886)... That night when Jesus made himself subject to weakness and suffering for love of me, he made me strong and courageous. He clothed me with his weapons and since that blessed night, I have not been conquered in any battle, but on the contrary have marched from victory to victory and started out, so to speak, on 'a giant's course' (Ms A 97).*

I had thought of calling this introduction *'A giant's course'*, for these words from Psalm 18:5 describe so well Thérèse's journey from her discovery of merciful Love which kindled her confidence and abandonment.[2] To understand just what she means when she says that she had *such confidence in Jesus' infinite Mercy* (Ms A 100), we have to understand her need for healing, that what she *had not been able to bring about in ten years, Jesus did in an instant, content with (her) good will which was never wanting* (Ms A 98).

Then *I felt charity come into my heart, the need to forget myself and to please others and since then I have been happy* (Ms A 99). This is the prelude to the ultimate invasion of merciful Love, after the act of Offering of 9 June 1895: *Ah! since that blessed day, it seems that Love possesses and surrounds me, it seems that at each moment this merciful Love is renewing me, purifying my soul and not leaving there any trace of sin* (Ms A 181). This Love which makes Jesus cry out on the cross: 'I thirst', resounds in her heart, and impels her to pray for sinners.

We cannot dwell at length on what Thérèse says of the effects of Love in her heart, but we do know that several days after she made her offering to Love, while she was making the Way of the Cross in Choir, 14 June 1895, she was seized with such an overwhelming love for God that had it lasted a few seconds longer, she would have died ... At least, we have here the key which enables us to understand why merciful Love could engulf her and this key also opens the door to the wound in Jacob's hip or the thorn in Paul's side.

This is why we must have great patience and compassion toward those who desire to love but who experience their

2 This book brings together thirteen short articles which appeared in *Vie Thérèsienne* from January 1978 to April 1984 centred round two of Thérèse's sayings which form the two sections of the book: *I will sing the mercies of the Lord* and *Now, abandonment alone guides me*. We have simply made these short articles chapters, giving them a title which did not appear in the original.

incapacity because of wounds caused by their sins, or because of the bruises made by their fellow human beings or, quite simply, because of their heredity. We must not discourage them but above all invite them, like Thérèse, to set out on this 'giant's course'. We must say to them: 'Go to the hospital for treatment before wishing to run Love's errands'.

To those who suffer from this lack of confidence – because it is confidence and nothing but confidence that leads to Love, as Thérèse again says – there is one word that we must not say to them. That word is 'courage', because this is precisely what they do not have. It would be like saying to someone who has no money: 'Pay! Pay!' We should rather say: 'Go to the source where you will receive bread and water ... without paying for it, freely. Go and be consoled and nourished. 'Come and buy for nothing' said the prophet Isaiah. There is a source which is free, it is that of merciful Love.

Conclusion: Pray for mercy ...

In concluding this introduction centred on Mercy and before entering into the contemplation of merciful Love put forward in these pages, I want to invite the reader to the prayer of humble petition. And I could do no better than go back to Pope John Paul's words, at the end of his Encyclical: *Dives in Misericordia, On the Mercy of God*. He says that all his teaching must be transformed into a cry that 'implores God's Mercy'.

'Everything that I have said in the present document on mercy should therefore be continually transformed into an ardent prayer: into a cry that implores mercy according to the needs of the modern world. May this cry be full of that truth about mercy which has found such rich expression in Sacred Scripture and in Tradition, as also in the authentic

15

life of faith of countless generations of the People of God. With this cry let us, like the sacred writers, call upon the God who cannot despise anything that he has made, that God who is faithful to himself, to his fatherhood and his love' (St Paul Publications, 84, 85).

Faced with God's mercy, we have nothing to offer but the cry of 'pleading poverty' which alone can touch the heart of the Father's mercy. 'To pray for mercy' (it is the Holy Father's expression) for ourselves and for all mankind should be the background of our prayer which is, according to Thérèse, the lever which lifts up the world in love (Ms C 258). In her act of Offering, Thérèse allows us to glimpse the essence of her prayer which consisted of praise, abandonment and petition.

When she contemplated merciful Love bending over each individual and humbly asking to be received, Thérèse herself began to pray that this Love might want to overflow into her heart. We have then an onslaught of petitions: the humble asking of God who begs human consent and Thérèse's prayer which is only made in response to God's:

In order to live in one act of perfect Love, I offer myself as a victim of holocaust to your merciful Love, humbly asking you to consume me unceasingly, allowing the waves of tenderness shut up in you to overflow into my soul so that I may in this way become a martyr of your Love, O my God (J. Clarke 277).

This is why the Autobiography ends with the humble prayer of the publican, who is, with the good thief and Mary Magdalene, the great master of prayer for our eastern Christian brothers and sisters. May Thérèse obtain for us a heart broken with repentance – the only disposition capable of touching the heart of the God of mercy – even if God has preserved us from sin. Then the real love of the Trinity,

16

incarnate in the heart of Christ and become for us merciful Love, will be able to flow freely in us:

I am not dashing to the first place, but to the last; rather than go up with the pharisee, I repeat, full of confidence, the publican's humble prayer. But most of all I imitate Mary Magdalene, her astounding or rather her loving boldness which delighted Jesus' heart captivates mine. Yes, I know that even if I had on my conscience all the sins that could be committed, I would go, my heart broken with sorrow and throw myself into Jesus' arms, for I know how much he loves the prodigal child who returns to him. It is not because God in his prevenient mercy has preserved my soul from mortal sin that I go to him with confidence and love ... (Ms C 259).

I

'I will sing the mercies of the Lord'

__1__

'Show us the face of your mercy'

Thérèse replied with some reticence to her sister Pauline's desire that she write the story of her soul. Her reticence is quite understandable: Thérèse was afraid that, in recounting it, she might put herself into the foreground by attracting attention to herself when God must always take first place. Men and women find their true greatness when kneeling, in second place. In spiritual literature too many tell about themselves instead of turning solely towards God. This is true in prayer, which for many becomes an appreciation of 'me' rather than a glance directed towards God and his merciful Love.

As always, Thérèse ponders over her sister Pauline's desire and Jesus makes her 'feel' in prayer that she will please him by obeying simply. Note in passing how Thérèse never lets herself be coerced from without: God's will comes to her from without, certainly, but it is always inscribed in the depths of her being, 'on the tablets of our heart'. In prayer, Thérèse 'felt' that by obeying her sister, she would please Jesus:

> *The day you asked me to do it, it seemed to me that my heart would become distracted by concentrating on myself, but Jesus has made me feel that by obeying simply I would please him; besides I am going to do only one thing: I am going to begin singing what I must sing for all eternity: 'The Mercies of the Lord'* (Ms A 13).

21

Vocation and mission

The starting point is clear. We do not have to rejoice in ourselves or to make a drama about our own person; what is important is God, his sanctity and above all his merciful Love. Thérèse knew that her ultimate vocation on earth and on the other side would be to sing eternally the mercies of the Lord. In this sense, her mission will continue in the next life and this is why 'she will spend her heaven doing good on earth', that is to say, helping men and women to place absolute confidence in God's mercy. She will never wear out her gaze contemplating mercy, as we wear out our eyes and our minds on earth trying to comprehend this deepest aspect of God, trying to understand his tenderness and his mercy.

By stating Thérèse's plan at the beginning of her writing, we will be restricting ourselves: we are not attempting a comprehensive study of God's mercy, or how Thérèse has sung, by modulation, the mercies of the Lord, but very simply we wish to push ajar some doors on this mystery. Faced with the mystery of mercy, we often feel that we should remain silent before these doors. So we try simply to remain in silence in front of these doors behind which there is someone who is knocking (Apoc. 3:20) and let the Holy Spirit push them ajar for us. We must allow this presence of God to be free in us and to lead us by the hand to the threshold of the mystery.

The goal of spiritual theology and Christian experience is the same, which amounts to saying that theology is useful to those who have already felt the impact of the thunderbolt of mercy. While the face of mercy does not demand our attention from within like a devouring fire, theological reflections on the mystery run the risk of leaving us with only the taste of ashes. This is why we are always apprehensive when it comes to speaking out about the climate of retreat prayer. As Karl Rahner said: 'Our theology will be a theology on our knees or it will not be.'

So we will devote this first section to approaching the climate of prayer which allowed Thérèse to sing the mercies of the Lord. Then we will apply ourselves to her perception of the Face of Mercy which she glimpsed in prayer, but at the same time we will look at how she saw her own face in relation to that of God. Indeed, it is impossible to discover God's mercy unless we are acutely aware of our own nothingness and our need to be saved.

Thérèse writes to pray

As soon as she says that she desires only to sing the mercies of the Lord, without becoming preoccupied with herself, Thérèse shows the climate of prayer in which she wished to write these pages. It gives us a practical guide as to how we should approach these short letters. Unless we do so in the same prayerful attitude we will run the risk of understanding nothing of Thérèse's thought:

> *Before taking up my pen, I knelt down before the statue of Mary (the one that has given so many proofs of the Queen of Heaven's maternal preferences for our family), I asked her to guide my hand so that I might not write one line displeasing her* (Ms A 13).

So it was in this spirit of prayer and intercession that Thérèse wanted to write down what the Spirit would prompt her to write. She did not write merely for the sake of writing, or to be read, but to pray. It is then a question of the prayer which placed her before God when she recalled God's grace at work in her so that she could spiritually retain it, and give thanks to God for it.

So she continued:

23

*Then, opening the holy Gospel, my eyes fell on these words:
'Jesus going up onto a mountain, called to him those whom
he desired, and they came to him' (Mk 3:13). That is the
mystery of my vocation, of my whole life and above all
the mystery of the privileges Jesus has showered on my soul
(Ms A 13).*

In this way Thérèse contemplates Jesus' privileges to her,
the mysterious ways he traces out in his creature to draw
it after him. The book of Thérèse's writings brings home
to us in a particular way how writing can help us to pray.
When Thérèse was looking at God's ways in her life she
never became introverted, but discovered in prayer the meaning of God's action in her regard.

By means of such prayer, which resembles the constant
gushing forth of a stream which is fed from the most mysterious depths of the heart, Thérèse touched the presence
and action of God within her and every moment of her
human destiny was transfigured by God's Mercy. Thérèse's
autobiographical manuscripts come to us as one of those
providential witnesses which show that we too can have an
interior life of prayer.

We often speak today of prayer in our life and of prayer
in action, without being too sure just what these words mean.
Thérèse bears special witness to that form of prayer which
is intended above all for apostles. Her prayer penetrates her
whole life as the rhythm of her breathing and the beats of
her heart animate her body. Here we are touching on the
great Eastern idea which is, that prayer should become part
of the two great rhythms of human life: the breathing and
the heart. It is a matter of bringing prayer from the mind
to the heart. For Thérèse prayer was the very source of her
existence and it is there that real union with God in action
takes place. It is something that goes on while we are living:

to experience God's presence and action in the very fabric of our own story.

Thérèse does not write to look at herself but to contemplate Jesus' privileges in her soul.

He does not call those who are worthy, but those whom he pleases or, as St Paul says: 'God will have mercy on whom he will have mercy, and he will have compassion on whom he will have compassion. So it does not depend then on man's will or effort, but upon God's mercy' (Rom 9:15,16).

The face of God's mercy

It is therefore not my life properly so called that I am going to write, it is my thoughts on the graces God has seen fit to grant me. I find myself at a period in my life when I can look back over the past: my soul has matured in the crucible of exterior and interior trials ... To me the Lord has always been compassionate and full of kindness ... Slow to punish and rich in mercy (Ps 102:8). So, Mother, I am happy that I am coming to sing near you the Mercies of the Lord' (Ms A 15).

When Thérèse looks back over her life, she acknowledges that God has always led her with gentleness: *'He leads me beside still waters. He revives my soul. He is compassionate and full of kindness'* (Ms A 15). And she first reads this mercy of God on the Face of Christ: *'Learn from me, says Jesus, for I am gentle and humble in heart, and you will find rest for your souls. Yes, my yoke is easy and my burden light* (Mt 11:29,30).

Prayer is essentially a personal encounter, an encounter between a person and God, but for it to be a genuine encounter the two persons must be truly themselves. Too often, truth is missing in our prayer because, instead of

25

turning to the living and true God, we address ourselves to something we imagine to be God. Thérèse sought the real face of God in truth and this is why her relationship with him was a reality.

We wonder then what face of God Thérèse encountered in prayer at the beginning of the manuscript; it must be said that it was the face of kindness, of tenderness and of mercy. She could have retained other faces, especially that of his justice, because she had been in contact with several Carmelites who had offered themselves to God's justice. Under the inspiration of the Holy Spirit, she understood that Jesus Christ is not the incarnation of any face of God, but the incarnation of his deepest and most mysterious face: his face of mercy. Jesus came on earth to show God's tenderness to those who are far off and afflicted.

It is not the healthy who need the doctor, but the sick. Go then and learn what this means: 'I want mercy, not sacrifice'. For I have come not to call the just, but sinners (Mt 9:12,13).

If we want to learn how to pray at the school of Thérèse, we have here a very important guide on how to go about it. The first thing we have to do at the beginning of prayer is to seek the true face of God, the only one which is revealed to us. Too often, a crowd of mental and visual images prevent us from meeting the true God.

We have drawn these reflections from our contacts with others, from our reading and even from our own personal experience; they are not exactly false, but they are inadequate for the reality of God. If we wish to encounter God as he really is, we must go to him with all our experiences and our knowledge but we have to renounce them in order to stand before God who is at once known and unknown. The only true prayer which then must rise, not only from our lips, but above all from the depths of our heart is: 'Show us, Lord, the true face of your mercy and we will be saved.'

God is free to reveal himself as he is

What will happen then? It is very simple. God who is free to come to us and show himself, to answer our prayer, will perhaps do so and we will then be aware of his presence and his gentleness, but he can also choose not to do so. We live 23 hours of our day without giving him a thought, it would then be a little out of place to ask him to show himself to us during the short hour that we devote to prayer.

And this is why we return to Thérèse and how she reacted at prayer when God was absent. She approaches prayer as she approaches writing, not seeking herself, but desirous only of pleasing God. She goes to prayer simply to be with Jesus and to sing again of his love; if he shows himself she rejoices, but she is not put out if he is absent.

We must never forget that aridity in prayer was Thérèse's daily bread. *I should be distressed for having slept (for seven years) during prayer and thanksgiving* (Ms A 165). This was a trial for the young Carmelite called to devote several hours each day to prayer. She goes even further and admits that Jesus was often absent from prayer and she uses the same humorous image of sleep: *Jesus was asleep as usual in the boat* (Ms A 165). Concerning this, Mgr Combes was to define, humorously, St Thérèse of Lisieux's prayer as 'the meeting of two sleepers': Jesus and Thérèse

So Thérèse experienced the apparent absence of God in her prayer and this experience is as important as the other, because in both cases, she touches on the reality of God's right to answer or to be silent. What mattered above all for Thérèse was to do God's will:

27

Today as yesterday, if it is possible, I have been deprived of all consolation. I thank Jesus who finds this good for my soul; perhaps if he consoled me, I would stop at the consolation, but he wants everything for himself! Well, everything is his, everything, even when I feel I have nothing to offer him, then as this evening, I will give him this nothing! ... If you knew the great joy that is mine when I have nothing to please Jesus! It is a subtle joy (not in the least felt) (LT 78).

In her prayer as in her relations with others, Thérèse makes a distinction between love and plain emotion. Too often we run the risk of surrounding both our prayer and our fraternal charity with this emotion. She wants to sing forever the mercies of the Lord and not recount her life's story. Returning to this aspect of Thérèse's prayer concerning her very arid profession retreat, we can understand better her acute perception of God's mercy and her own nothingness.

2

Thérèse discovers mercy

Thérèse, at grips with arduous prayer, gradually learns to love God for himself and for himself alone. Let us return to the eve of her profession after two-and-a-half years of religious life. She tells us how she spent that retreat and before describing the geography of her spiritual journey, she first states her goal.

The summit of the mountain of love

> But the little hermit will tell you the itinerary of her journey. Here it is. Before setting out, her fiancé seemed to ask her in what country she wished to travel, what route she wished to follow, etc. The little fianceé said that she had but one desire and that was to be taken to the summit of the mountain of love (LT 110).

There is no mistaking Thérèse's desire, her sights are set on the summit of love, that is, the unconditional gift of herself to merciful Love which is hidden from her. But the paths which lead to the summit are many, Jesus knows that she wants to climb the mountain, but Thérèse allows him to choose the path. Since she has undertaken the journey for him alone, she lets herself be led by the ways Jesus likes to go. *As long as he is satisfied, I am completely happy.*

For Thérèse the fullness of joy consists in fulfilling Jesus' desire. A person becomes truly lovable the moment he or she no longer lives for themselves but is completely poured out in another. It is a kind of disappearance of a person's will into the will of God. And I think this is the only definition of prayer, of conversation with God: to-be-poured-out-into-another. It is the image of the trinitarian dialogue where Jesus is totally poured out in his Father. One of the basic tests of real prayer is seeking God before seeking self. Thérèse expresses herself in this way:

> *Then Jesus took my hand and made me enter a subterranean passage where it is neither cold nor hot, where the sun does not shine and neither rain nor wind visit; a subterranean passage where I see nothing but a half-veiled light, the light which comes from the lowered eyes of my fiancé's face!*
>
> *My fiancé says nothing to me, and I say nothing to him, except that I love him more than myself, I feel in the depths of my heart that this is true, for I am more his than my own.*
>
> *I do not see that we are going towards the summit of the mountain, since we are travelling underground, however it seems to me that we are nearing it, without my knowing how.*
>
> *The route has no consolations for me and yet it brings me all consolations since Jesus chose it and I want to console him alone, only him!* (LT 110).

Christ is always at the centre of Thérèse's prayer; it does not matter what she feels or that the tunnel she walks along is dark, the important thing is to love him. Little by little, Thérèse abandons herself and walks with her hand in Jesus' hand, without knowing where she is going. She does not see the path clearly but she is guided by Jesus' compass. She knows in whom she has put her trust' (2 Tim 1:12). The expressions Thérèse uses clearly show this: *I love him (Jesus) more than myself ... I desire to console him alone.* In the depths of her heart she knows very well that this is the way Jesus wishes for her: *I feel in the depths of my heart that it is true, for I am more his than my own.*

I will sing ...

Released from herself, from her impressions and her anxieties, Thérèse can sing the mercies of the Lord. She is truly humble because she is captivated by the face of God's tenderness. It is said of Moses that after he had contemplated the burning bush, he was the most humble man on earth (Num 12:3). This is not surprising: anyone who has seen God can no longer be preoccupied with anything but singing of his holiness and his mercy.

Above, Thérèse said that she saw *only a half-veiled light, the light which comes from the lowered eyes of her fiancé's face.* One day Thérèse wrote to her sister, Céline: *When Jesus casts his glance on a soul, the latter can no longer tear itself away, and it must not for a single moment cease looking at him.* Thérèse will be faithful to keeping her gaze fixed on Jesus. When she was about six or seven years old, she said:

I have taken the resolution never to take my soul away from Jesus' gaze. Concerning her first Communion, she wrote: *Jesus and the poor little Thérèse looked at each other and understood each other ... That day, there was no longer one look but a fusion, there were no longer two, Thérèse had disappeared like a drop of water lost in the ocean. Jesus alone remained. He was Master* (Ms A, 77).

If we want to understand Thérèse's prayer of praise, we must pause in prayer at those moments where she says that she glimpsed God's merciful gaze shining in the Holy Face. We will return to it in the following paragraph. But for the moment we will let Thérèse sing about her discovery. She was well aware that God had given her many gifts, but instead of appropriating them to herself, she returns them to the author of every good gift. I think this is *to give thanks and sing the mercies of the Lord.*

The truly humble of heart is one who knows that he or she has received much from God, but who is forthwith captivated by him. Such a person does not stop at self, is freed from egotism and does not waste time ruminating over his or her miseries as joys. And in this way the person is delivered from all the complications of life. We are a long way here from superiority and inferiority complexes which come from the same root: self-introspection. Thérèse expresses it this way:

> *It seems to me that if a little flower could speak, it would say quite simply what God has done for it, without trying to hide its benefits. Under the pretext of a false humility, it would not say that it was without beauty or perfume, that the sun had taken away its splendour and storms had broken its stem, when it knew that this was not so. The flower which is going to tell her story rejoices to make known Jesus' totally gratuitous gifts. She knows that she has nothing to attract his divine glances and that his mercy alone is responsible for all the good in her* (Ms A 15).

In this sense, Thérèse is indeed the sister of the Blessed Virgin. She had an acute awareness of the gifts the Saviour had given her, and she proclaims in her eternal Magnificat: *The Lord has done marvels for me, Holy is his Name ... His mercy is from age to age to those who fear him.* Thérèse, like the Virgin, proclaims that God alone is important, that his gifts are free and that the only fitting response is to sing the wonders of the Lord.

In that, she fully realises the definition St Paul gives to the Christian life: *Rejoice always. In all things, give thanks, pray unceasingly* (1 Thess 5:15,16). In the spiritual life, the continual prayer to which we are called is joined to continual thanksgiving. The essence of the Christian life – and even more so for the Carmelite – is to sing the mercies of the Lord, in a word, our life is a thanksgiving liturgy. Humanity pours out its strength in libation to give joy to God and proclaims it with all its strength.

Thérèse is very much in line with the Jewish liturgy which places the prayer of blessing at the centre of worship. We have somewhat lost this meaning of the prayer of benediction by reducing it to 'blessings' given to persons or things. To bless God, that is to speak of his goodness (*bene = good; dicere = to speak*), is to rejoice purely and simply in his existence. To bless God is also to thank him for all the good he has done for us (prayer of thanksgiving); it is also to praise him for all the gifts which he is ready to give us provided we make him the gift of our prayer of petition (and that is the prayer of intercession). I am struck today by the fact that Christians are instinctively rediscovering this form of prayer especially in renewal groups and they are all unanimous in saying that they experience the power of praise.

What is mercy?

Thérèse recounts 'the good deeds' of the Lord, she 'makes known Jesus' totally gratuitous gifts' to her. With Thérèse there is no attempt to assess her own merits. In other words, she plays at the bank of love where there is no ledger for accounts. *She knows that she had nothing to attract his divine glances and that his mercy alone is responsible for all the good in her* (Ms A 15).

Before continuing our study, it is good to ask what kind of love does Thérèse want to sing. For her, it was not a question of just any sort of love, but of '*only God's mercy*'. It is clearly spelt out in the text we have just quoted and

Thérèse defines the love she wants to sing thus: *The attribute of love is to humble itself.*

This is not always the case in human relationships. When we love a friend for example, he or she is not inferior to us; on the contrary, we love that person because of the qualities we find in them. We know that condescension, which is sometimes a form of pity that makes one go out to the unfortunate, is often dangerous for it opens the door to all sorts of deviations: paternalism, maternalism, etc.

But when God loves his creature, it is essentially 'a love between two unequal beings where the greater stretches out his hand to the smaller. God binds himself to humanity and makes mutual love possible' (Conrad de Meester, *With Empty Hands*). And there, Thérèse touches on an essentially biblical intuition: the mercy and the tenderness of God. The Lord our God is the God of tenderness and pity, slow to anger and full of mercy. In Hebrew, there are no abstract words to designate this love, the expression is very concrete: the maternal womb; the bowels of mercy.

In biblical terms, this love will become *'Hesed'* which calls forth from humanity gratitude, acceptance and reciprocity. In the New Testament vocabulary, and more especially in St Paul, it is a question of grace *(charis).* The angel Gabriel greets Mary: *Rejoice, full of grace*; which comes back to saying: *'God has looked on you with so much tenderness and mercy that his love has made you lovable and pleasing in his sight'.*

This is why I can say that Mary had the charism of the Magnificat, the charism of the lowly ones who sing the mercies of God for the little people and the poor. In this sense, Mary's prayer, like that of Thérèse, is the opposite to that of the pharisee in the Gospel. He thanks God that he is not like the rest of humanity. Mary also thanks God that she is different from others, but for the very simple reason that she is poor and a little one, and in this way she joins here directly the prayer of the publican.

The only prayer capable of moving God's heart is always that of the publican in the Gospel. There is a liturgical text which expresses this very well, it is the Magnificat antiphon for the second Vespers of the Common of the Blessed Virgin: 'Rejoice with me, all you who love the Lord; in my lowliness, I have pleased the most High'. In Latin, the text is even stronger: *'Ego placui Altissimo cum essem parvula'*, *'I have pleased the most High because I was so lowly'*. We will come back to that. Mary gave thanks because she had been protected from contracting sin, which, according to Thérèse, is the ultimate pardon. Thérèse herself will say:

> *I know that without him (God) I could have fallen as low as St Mary Magdalene, and the Lord's profound words to Simon resound with great sweetness in my soul, the one to whom less is forgiven, LOVES less, but I know that Jesus has forgiven me more than St Mary Magdalene, since he forgave me in advance, by preventing me from falling. Ah, if only I could put into words what I feel! Here is an example which will express my thought at least a little* (Ms A 83,84).

Thérèse then goes on to tell the parable of the doctor who removed the stone from the path where his son had to pass, without the latter seeing him. Thérèse, like Mary, had the understanding that she had been pardoned before coming into contact with sin and this is why they both have what I call the charism of the Magnificat. This is also why it can be said that Thérèse is the Blessed Virgin's sister because she is the echo of her voice for the men and women of our day.

Thérèse did not write to instruct but to recount the marvels of God, and she very quickly understood that she was writing for the little ones, the poor and the weak who were afraid to have confidence in God. Then, as she too had the folly of the Blessed Virgin's confidence, she felt that she had to sing the mercies of the Lord to the tone of the Magnificat.

'I have pleased the Most High because I was so lowly'

And this brings us to mercy's last defence. The background, as one would say, of God's merciful love is that God is attracted by our poverty and need, but it must also be added that we are fascinated by God's splendour and beauty. The Bible sings for us in all tones this love that God has for the little and the weak: *If the Lord set his love on you and chose you, it was not because you were the most numerous of all the peoples. But it was out of love of you and to keep the oath he swore to your fathers* (Deut 7:7-8). All the Old Testament is a jealous wrangle between God and his people who do not respond to his love. And yet God had pity on his adulterous spouse whom he found by the wayside, soaked in her blood.

Speaking of mercy, Paul Claudel said: 'It is not an offhanded giving of things that we no longer need, it is a passion'. *(Cinq grandes odes: La Maison fermée.)* In this sense, it can be said that God's heart is ravaged by the passion of mercy, it is God's suffering in the face of those who waste or fail to recognise his love. When the Bible speaks of God's anger, it is speaking in another way of this passion of love which makes a turn around before one who is hardened. But in the end, God is always moved with pity for his anger does not last. In his *Homily on Ezechiel* (6:6), Origen speaks of this loving passion of God which runs counter to the rational timidity of the wise of this world. In this way Origen affirms that 'in his love for us, the impassable One suffered a passion of mercy.

36

'What is this passion that he has first undergone for us? It is the passion of love.

'But the Father himself, God of the Universe, who is full of forebearance, mercy and pity, is it that he does not suffer as it were? or are you quite unaware that, when he is concerned with human things, he suffers human passion? *For the Lord your God has taken on himself your ways, as a father takes up his son* (Deut 1, 31). God therefore takes on himself our ways, as the Son of God takes our passions. The Father himself is not impassable! If we pray to him, he has pity and compassion. He suffers a passion of love.'

Our misery and our suffering so moved God's heart with sympathy that he became incarnate in Jesus Christ to show us his most mysterious face, that is to say, the face of his mercy. The mystery of mercy is the wound in God's heart caused by those who become lost. As the Bible often repeats, it is the overthrow of the bowels of mercy:

> *I have seen my people's misery in Egypt. I have heard their cry before their oppressors; yes, I know their anguish. I have come down to save them from the land of the Egyptians* (Ex 3:7-8).

And when Moses prayed to God to show him his glory (Ex 33:18), he revealed himself as *the Lord, the Lord, a God of tenderness and pity, slow to anger, rich in steadfast love and fidelity, keeping steadfast love for thousands, forgiving iniquity, transgression and sin, but who will leave nothing unpunished* (Ex 34:6-8). When Paul will speak of this mystery hidden from all ages, he says: *God did not make known to people of past generations this mystery as it has now been revealed by the Spirit to his apostles and prophets* (Eph 3:5). To understand this passion of God, reread the story of the prodigal son, the drachma, the lost sheep where it is said that God experiences joy when he finds his child again.

We have to understand this principle which impels God to have a weakness for what is little and poor in order to understand why Mary pleased the most High, and why he filled her with his gifts: her immaculate conception, divine maternity, assumption etc. God freely loved Mary, but as one theologian, Fr Molinié, has rightly said, if God's love is free, it is not arbitrary, that is to say, that there was then something in Mary which attracted God's heart and which he could not resist. In other words, Mary offered God a heart that was poor, humble and above all boundlessly confident — an absolutely free space — where his Word could become flesh. It was Mary's poverty, humility and confidence that pleased the most High.

Thérèse's instinct about mercy

Thérèse's inspired intuition was to understand the depth of God's heart, with regard to mercy. Thérèse understood the merciful heart of God, as St Paul understood the mystery of Christ. And they both reached the same contemplation of God who is merciful. Thérèse cites explicitly this text in her manuscripts (Ms A 13): *It does not depend on a person's will or efforts, but on God's mercy* (Rom 9:16).

And this inspired discovery will give rise in a person's heart to a simple movement of confidence in Jesus, the only Saviour: *We are not justified by practising the law, but by faith in Jesus Christ* (Gal 2:16). We understand then how our Protestant brothers and sisters are in mutual agreement about confidence in mercy, which is proper to Thérèse of Lisieux.

I have often asked myself how Thérèse was able to understand the heart of God with such clarity and to be fascinated by his mercy. It seems to me that the answer is simple: God made her understand to what extent he loved her and how much he desired to be loved by her. Jesus gave her *the grace to understand more than ever before how much* (he) *desired to be loved* (Ms A 180).

This was a dazzling intense light for Thérèse. In other words, she had seen the face of God's mercy. I often think of her when I read these words of Silouane: 'The Lord is merciful; my soul knows this, but it is not possible to put it into words. He is infinitely gentle and humble and if the soul sees him, it is transformed into him, it becomes all love for its neighbour, it too becomes humble and gentle.'

The only way to understand God's mercy is to have a certain likeness to him, an affinity which makes us sharers in his desires and his ways. When we are like someone, we very easily predict what they are going to think and do. If Thérèse had an instinct about God's mercy, it was because God's merciful love had flooded her heart. As soon as God's charity began to burn in her and consume her, she was affected by mercy which made her grasp that folly of the cross.

On this subject of mercy which is inexhaustible, it could be said that Thérèse expresses her desires:

Jesus, Jesus, if I wanted to write down all my desires, I would have to borrow your book of life where the deeds and works of all your saints are recorded, and I would accomplish them all for you (Ms B 193).

The important thing is to pray to Thérèse fervently and ask her to give us some experience in the depths of our hearts of the power, the gentleness and the folly of mercy.

In the following chapter we will come back again to her perception of mercy but at the same time stressing still more her perception of her own nothingness. Finally we will attempt to approach this movement of confidence which is the characteristic proper to Theresian spirituality. I am writing these lines on 1 October, the feast of St Thérèse of Lisieux and I have reread these last words in silence and prayer. They confirm in reality her discovery of merciful love and her intuition about humility:

> *Yes, it seems to me that I have never sought anything but the truth; yes, I have understood humility of heart. It seems to me that I am humble.*
>
> *All that I have written about my desires for suffering! Oh! It is true just the same.*
>
> *... And I do not regret having surrendered myself to Love. Oh! no, I do not regret it, on the contrary* (LC 30.9).

3

Thérèse discovers her own nothingness

To understand Thérèse, as we have said before, we need to have a certain affinity with her. When we are like someone, we understand what they are thinking, what they are saying and what they are doing. As soon as mercy begins to burn in the heart of a man or a woman, they are in danger of becoming Thérèse's brother or sister. She was not always understood in her Carmel and more than one sister thought that in the divine order, justice took precedence over mercy. But Thérèse was not to be put off and knew how to stand firm. She said to one of her sisters: *Sister, you want justice, well, you will get justice! As for me, I choose mercy!* And she added: *We obtain from God exactly what we expect from him.*

An affinity with Thérèse

So in order to understand Thérèse, we need to have experienced a groundswell that upturns our boat and that groundswell is mercy. It is not something we can invent or produce ourselves, it is the invasion within us of the deepest feeling of God's heart. As Fr Molinié rightly says, mercy is the look someone who is in heaven casts on another who is not there. It is Jesus' attitude towards the good thief: *This evening, you will be with me in paradise.* On this subject, let us say that Céline sometimes spoke of her sister Thérèse's 'way of the good thief'.

And I can understand why men and women in the 20th century have a certain affinity with Thérèse. Our contemporaries are only too well aware of their finiteness and their poverty. The further humanity advances in its discoveries the more it realises that it is in second place, and it experiences its solitude. This is why the desire for tenderness and gentleness is emerging among young people. Look at the press and you will see how these words of tenderness and gentleness are appearing on every line of the articles because the young are obsessed by them. You could say that our contemporaries are discovering through this cold and lonely world that we need the look, the face and the companionship of another.

In this sense, I think that Thérèse answers the desire and expectation of the men and women of today and more especially the young who are starving for tenderness. There is an affinity between them and Thérèse, even if their vocabulary and mode of thought are not the same. Thérèse is thinking of them explicitly when she speaks of the different types of souls who are attracted by a perfection of God:

> I understand however that all souls are not alike. It is necessary that there are different types so that each of God's perfections might be honoured in a special way. To me he has given his infinite mercy and it is through it I contemplate and adore this other divine perfections! All these seem to me to be resplendent with love, even justice (and this perhaps even more than any other) seems to be clothed with love (Ms A 180).

The further I go the more I believe that there is a similarity and unity between the spiritualities, especially when you return to their source. Fundamentally, St John of the Cross, like St Ignatius and St Francis of Assisi, drew their spirituality from the living source of the Gospel. The point of departure is an encounter with the face of Jesus Christ, a turning towards him and an adopting of the ways of the Son of God. This comes back to saying that the beatitudes, the spirit of childhood, the following of Christ in carrying his cross, and humility form the basis of all the spiritualities. It is enough to look at St Benedict's Rule to understand how humility is central to the monk's experience, although there might be 12 degrees that we cannot understand very well.

On the other hand, if I do not believe so much in particular spiritualities, I do believe very strongly in types of souls and spiritual affinities between a saint and a person who is still a pilgrim on this earth. If I were to ask a friend of Thérèse or a disciple of St John of the Cross why they loved them, they possibly could not give me a rational answer. On this subject, Montaigne's words come to my mind when he was asked his reasons for his friendship with La Boétie, he replied simply: 'Because he was who he was and I was who I was!'

There, everything is clear and each one has his or her place. Undoubtedly it would have been necessary to have covered a great distance in search of an ideal of sanctity, glimpsed in adolescence, still pursued and never attained, to understand how one was a brother or sister of Thérèse in a similar spiritual adventure. Let us go even further and admit that as we grow older we are forced to admit that it is beyond our strength. Let us say that it is within our capacity to desire it but that it is not within our capacity to realise it.

And it is here that Thérèse comes back to us and says: 'Now you are ready to understand mercy!' And she continues the text we have cited above:

What a joy it is to think that God is just, that he understands perfectly our frail human nature. What then should I fear? Ah! The infinitely just God who deigns to pardon with

43

so much kindness the faults of the prodigal son, must he not be just also towards me who 'am with him always' (Lk 15:32) (Ms A 180).

The mountain or the grain of sand

Bernanos said: 'It is often a leap taken in despair that throws us into hope and confidence!' These words can be applied to the letter to Thérèse. She truly understood God's mercy and sang it by bringing together the deepest dimension of her nothingness and her poverty. Whatever the discovery of this nothingness might have been – since Thérèse admits that she had never refused God anything since the age of three – we must take her words literally. Thérèse had indeed been protected from sin – she herself says so – but that did not prevent her from discovering a deeper misery than moral misery, which I will call her ontological 'misery' which is her deficiency of being. In a word, she understood that she was in second place and that it was morally necessary for her to humbly fall on her knees.

We could compare Thérèse's discovery to an experience of the Curé of Ars. One day he had asked God to show him his nothingness. God heard his prayer and he was given such light on the contingency of his being, entirely dependent upon God's mercy that he said: 'If God had not sustained me I could have then imagined a temptation to despair.' And he advised his penitents against ever making such a prayer.

'I am the One who is', Christ said one day to Catherine of Siena, 'and you are she who is not'. All the saints had to pass through this experience which plunges them into the most radical humility, as Job was beaten into the dust. I think that the first degree of humility is to recognise that God has first place and that we are in the second, and this places the necessity of prayer and supplication in their right place in

44

our life. 'To know oneself, to know God! That is our perfection. On the one hand, all immensity, all perfection and absolute goodness; and on the other, nothing; to know that is our end. To be eternally over this twofold abyss: that is my secret', said St Angela de Foligno.

It is therefore in this perspective that we have to understand the text that we are going to cite now in its entirety. But firstly we must put it into its historical context and, above all, in Thérèse's spiritual journey towards sanctity. On 14 September, after having cared for her father, Céline entered the Lisieux Carmel at the time when Thérèse was painfully experiencing her own nothingness; let us say rather of the interior discrepancy between a real desire for sanctity and the established fact of her powerlessness to attain it. She could have said like St Paul: *I fail to carry out the things I want to do* (Rom 7:15).

This is a crucial time in the life of a man or woman in search of God and will determine whether it will be yes or no to setting out towards real or a fanciful sanctity. Two solutions can then present themselves: either sanctity is seen to be an impossibility and they invest all their energies in the immediate here and now, in what is tangible; or they make a radical acceptance of the humility of their human condition and plunge solely into God in confidence. But for this to happen a word of God must come and enlighten them on the mystery of God's mercy in the face of humanity's nothingness.

For Thérèse, this word of God was to come from her sister Céline who entered Carmel with a note-book which would play an important role, said Conrad de Meester. Céline had recopied into a small note-book a number of texts all on the subject of humility and the spirit of childhood (Is 66:12-13; Mt 18:1 etc.). Let us quote simply the most significant: *Whoever is a little one, let him come to me* (Prov 9:4). Thérèse

45

became aware of these texts at the end of 1894 or the beginning of 1895. We can then understand the context in which she made her act of offering to Merciful Love on 9 June 1895. She had needed that long preparation to understand that God was much more interested in her poverty than in the great virtues she could have offered him. Let us not forget that Thérèse wrote down this text a few months before her death and so it is enriched by the experience of the two last years. Let us cite it in its entirety, it merits being learnt by heart:

You know, Mother, that I have always wanted to be a saint. But alas, I have always noticed, when I compare myself to the saints, that between them and me there is the same distance that exists between a mountain whose summit is lost in the clouds and the obscure grain of sand trodden underfoot by passers-by. Instead of becoming discouraged, I said: 'God would not inspire unrealisable desires, I can therefore despite my littleness aspire to sanctity. It is impossible for me to grow up, so I must bear with myself such as I am with all my imperfections. But I am going to look for a means of going to heaven by a little way that is very direct, very short and totally new' (Ms A 207).

'I must bear with myself such as I am'

First, Thérèse reaffirms her desire to be a saint. On this point there can be no misunderstanding. From her earliest childhood, she has aspired to sanctity. Let us remark in passing, that this sanctity is realistic, that is it must be worked out in the very fabric of her existence and in the poor milieu of the Carmel: *Illusions*, said Thérèse, *God gave me the grace not to have any when I entered Carmel. I found religious life to be just what I had imagined it, no sacrifice surprised me* (Ms A 149).

When we come into contact with the harsh reality, our desire for sanctity loses its edge and there is always the risk

46

for all of us of giving up and saying: 'It is impossible'.
Thérèse will be confronted with her personal powerlessness.
On the one hand there is her desire (the mountain whose
summit is lost in the clouds) and the reality (that is to say
the grain of sand trodden underfoot by the passers-by). But
it is here that she will react differently and instead of sacrific-
ing her ideal for reality, she will search for sanctity starting
with her human condition and her everyday life. The more
she will face events, poor and unable, the more she will
abandon herself to Jesus Christ, the incarnation of God's
mercy.

This is why instead of being discouraged, she will hold
together, cost what may, her littleness and her aspiration
to sanctity. And the key-word here appears in this sentence: *I must bear with myself such as I am with all my
imperfections!* To the degree that she fully accepts that she
is a poverty-stricken and fundamentally inadequate creature
will she discover simultaneously that mercy is there to fill
her. Mercy will not be for her an attribute of God, but her
very being.

So, starting with her actual life and her poverty offered
to God, a dialogue will be established between one who is
and one who is not. It is here that Thérèse rejoices that she
is a child of God singing his mercies, and at the same time
rejoices in her nothingness by accepting it with joy. Furthermore, she learns, as she will later tell her sister Céline, to
discover her poverty as a precious pearl to love and worth
all the searching: *You must love sweetly your misery!*

A lift or the rough stairway of perfection

And yet she will never sacrifice her desire to go to heaven
to the harsh reality of her own nothingness and it is here
that the inspired discovery of the lift appears:

We are living in an age of inventions, and we no longer have to go to the trouble of climbing a staircase; in the homes of the rich, a lift has successfully replaced it. I would like to find a lift that would take me up to Jesus, for I am too small to climb the rough stairway of perfection (Ms A 207).

On this point, I am not afraid to say that this discovery of a lift is inspired, but we must also look at the other part of the antithesis, that is, the 'rough stairway of perfection'. Thérèse was living in an age when 'plans of perfection' were proposed to her *(Dom André Louf)*. For many spiritual writers, there was a starting-point: above there was heaven and perfection; below, at the foot of the stairway, was weak frail humanity. Between the two it was necessary to throw a bridge or, as Thérèse said, a lift. So perfection was often thought of and described as a continual progression, or a more or less arduous ascent which was the fruit of the individual's effort. In this case, all ascetical technique was based on generosity. At the end of the ascent the effort opened itself into liberty.

And it is there that Thérèse understood just how the 'rough stairway of perfection' followed a track that was exactly opposite to that of the holy Gospel. Jesus himself expressed that opposition strongly and with few words in a little sentence which constantly recurs in the Gospel: *Whoever exalts himself will be humbled; and whoever humbles himself will be exalted* (Mt 23:12; Lk 14:11, 18:14). These two kinds of spiritual paths are personified in the persons of the Pharisee and the Publican, in the parable set in the Temple.

The first represents the 'rough stairway of perfection', which is in the end a natural, humanistic and secular perfection. The second symbolised by 'the lift' represents the profoundly Christian approach which is that of repentance. This latter is never within the individual's capability, but is always the fruit of a gratuitous election and a marvel of mercy and grace.

By constantly looking at heaven and closely examining the secrets of mercy, Thérèse understood that there was no ladder to take her above, but there was a lift that God alone could bring down. And she had to be vigilant, waiting and on the look-out for the arrival of the lift.

Simone Weil wrote in *Waiting for God*: 'We are unable to take even one step towards heaven. The vertical direction prevents us. But if we look at heaven for a long time, God comes down and lifts us up. He lifts us up easily. As Aeschyles says: 'What is divine is without effort ...' In the Gospel parables, God is the seeker: *quaerens me sedisti lassus*. Nowhere in the Gospel do we find the search undertaken by an individual. No one takes a step unless they are pushed or else explicitly called'.

This is why Thérèse searched in the lives of the saints and collected all that she could find about the little ones God carries in his arms: *As a mother caresses her child, so will I console you, you will be carried at the breast and I will fondle you on my knees* (Is 66: 12-13). Thérèse no longer had to count on her generosity or her ascetical efforts but to lean only on God's mercy, symbolised by the lift. She then proceeds to comment on the words of Isaiah:

> *Ah! never did words more tender or more melodious come to bring joy to my soul, the lift which must take me up to heaven are your arms, Jesus! And so I do not have to grow up, on the contrary, I must remain little, and I must become more and more so. O God, you have surpassed my expectation and I want to sing of your mercies. You have taught me from my youth and until now I have told of your marvels, and I will continue to make them known in old age (Ps 70:17-18)* (Ms C 208).

It is indeed in the context of the lift and of God's mercy that Thérèse sings his marvels. Thérèse has only one desire: to please Jesus: *For a long time, she has understood that God*

needs no one (still less her than others) to do good on earth
(Ms C 208).

To give without counting ...
but it is very little ...

We must not therefore think that Thérèse is encouraging a
certain quietism on our part. She will never overlook the part
played by personal co-operation but she puts it in its right
place, at the service of confidence and abandonment. We do
what we can, not to force God nor to snatch from his hands
strength for ourselves, but in order to experience our own
poverty and weakness. Once we have done all the good works
within our power, we will quickly discover that we are unprofitable servants. When tired and exhausted we will be able to
hear Jesus' word and experience the sweetness of his mercy:
Come to me all you who are weary, (from trying to bear the
burden of the Law), *and I will teach you gentleness and humility.*
Thérèse expressed it in these words to her sister Céline:

> *We must do all in our power, she said, to give without count-
> ing, to deny ourselves constantly, in a word, to prove our love
> by all the good works in our power. But truly, how very little
> is all this ... Even when we have done all that we think we
> ought to do, we must admit that we are 'unprofitable servants'*
> (Lk 17:10), nevertheless hoping that God will give us,
> through his grace, all that we desire. This is the hope of
> the little souls who 'run' in the way of childhood: I said
> 'run' and not 'rest' (CSG).

In this way courage, generosity and personal effort are put
in their rightful place. As Thérèse said: *how very little is all
this* which comes back to saying that they are a weak con-
tribution. Asceticism will lead very quickly to a neutral
position where old habits refuse to assist and give way before
what it painfully felt to be humanly impossible.

50

In this we must recognise that Thérèse is one here with the purest intuition of the former monks of the desert. They are often presented as champions of achievement and asceticism which were thought to be the goal of the spiritual life. For them, asceticism leads the monk to the neutral position where he can do no more than have confidence in God. 'Of what value are fasts and vigils?' asked an old monk to Abba Moses. The latter replied: 'They have no other effect than making a man humble. If the soul produces this fruit, God's bowels (the bowels of mercy) are moved for his sake.'

One of the oldest witnesses of this experience is undoubtedly Macarius the Great. He is one of the first in the monastic tradition to have treated explicitly the spiritual experience. In his *Little Letter* called *Ad Filios Dei*, he explores this theme at length. When the heart is as it were 'wilted', and 'it has almost yielded to temptations' God steps in and sends him 'holy strength':

'The benevolent God finally opens the eyes of the heart so that it understands that he alone is allowing it to stand. The individual can then truly give glory to God (that is to say, sing the Lord's mercies) in all humility and contrition … Humility, contrition, docility and gentleness come from the difficulty of the struggle.'

'It is your arms, O Jesus!'

Whatever we might do, it is God who makes us holy provided that we want to come to Jesus and offer him our poverty. The lift is God's mercy coming down to our powerlessness. God who is infinitely tender, contemplates human suffering through the disfigured face of his Son Jesus on the Cross.

On our side, we have to fully accept our misery, which implies profound humility. This means that before becoming humble and little, we must accept carrying our cross lamentably.

We find this repugnant for we want to carry our cross generously and gloriously, which is the exact opposite to carrying our cross humbly and poorly. On this subject we have two beautiful texts written by Thérèse to her sister Céline:

Why be afraid that you cannot carry this cross without weakness? Jesus, on the road to Calvary fell three times, and you, poor little child, you would not be like your Spouse, you would not be willing to fall a hundred times, if needs be, to prove your love for him by rising, with greater strength than before your fall (LT 81).

We would wish to suffer generously, nobly ... what an illusion! We would never want to fall? – What does it matter, Jesus, if I fall at each moment, it shows me my weakness and for this reason is a great gain for me. It shows you what I am able to do and now you will be more tempted to carry me in your arms (it is still the lift). *If you do not do it, it is because it pleases you to see me on the ground. Then I am not going to be disturbed, but I shall always stretch out my arms to you in supplication and full of love! I cannot believe that you would abandon me!* (LT 89).

Sanctity is therefore seen always as a tension between two poles: God infinitely merciful and humanity poor and powerless. Thérèse confesses her need and acknowledges that God is the one who, with mercy, comes to her aid. Jesus' arms are drawing her towards the Father, the source of all sanctity. This was to give rise in her to a twofold attitude: her offering to merciful Love and blind confidence in this same love. This attitude overflowed in loving abandonment to Jesus. But to understand this, it is necessary to take literally Jesus' advice:

Come to me, all you who are labouring beneath the load of the burden and I will give you rest (the letting go in *abandonment*). *Take my yoke upon you and learn from me, for I am gentle and humble of heart and you will find rest for your souls. Yes, my yoke is easy to carry and my burden light* (Mt 11:28-30).

4

The act of offering to merciful love

At the end of 1894, when she was confronted by the sight of her poverty, Thérèse discovered at the same time the mystery of mercy. This discovery is also the fruit of something perceived, as St Paul said to the Galatians: *I have publicly portrayed Christ on the Cross before your eyes* (Gal 3:1). Until 9 June 1895, the day when she made her act of offering, the Holy Spirit had been at work in prayer to bring her to this decisive act in her spiritual life.

Perhaps it is useful to note here a study by Mgr Combes entitled: *'Ma vocation, c'est l'amour'*. It was a talk given on 30 May 1965 at the Cenacle at Breteuil. It would take too long and be impossible to summarise this text but let us say that the author uses the method of historical criticism. He shows from texts 'the mystery of this supreme moment in the spiritual progress made by St Thérèse of Lisieux which is written down in a famous, well-known and important text, but which and this is the extraordinary thing, no one has ever expounded'.

The author asks us to make 'a considerable mental effort to try and examine closely this veritable mystery'. He goes on to develop a thesis which he has never ceased defending and which places the act of offering to merciful Love at the centre of Theresian spirituality. For him, the expression 'way of childhood' never came from Thérèse's pen and it was developed by the milieu in which she lived. Since Conrad de Meester has given us a major study *Dynamique de la Confidence*, popularised in his book *With Empty Hands*, we can understand better that these two view-points do not exclude each other but rather are linked together as we have tried to show in the preceding pages. However André Combes' study is very illuminating for our subject today and we strongly recommend it to our readers.

But we will return to 1895, the time when Thérèse was preparing to make her act of offering. And so as to understand better the impact and consequences of this step in Thérèse's life, let us take a leap to July 1897, when her sister was collecting her last words *(Her Last Conversations)*. Thérèse's word seems to me to be very important, for she puts us in contact with what happened after 9 June 1895. In other terms we are putting our finger on the effects of the act of offering to mercy and what is taking place in the heart of a person who is face to face with merciful Love.

'... As if I had been totally plunged into fire ...'

If there was ever a life seemingly without exterior phenomena, it was the life of Thérèse! Yet it must be said that Thérèse did have an authentic mystical experience, that is to say that she not only lived merciful Love in a hidden and underground way, but she experienced the power of that love within her. She was keenly aware of it and knew those states described by St Teresa of Avila and many of the saints (she herself notes this).

I think that her death of love on 30 September 1897 is the completion of this awareness, on the level of 'spiritual consciousness', of that invasion of merciful Love in her. She had a very clear perception of being transpierced through and through by a sword of love. That was how she explained it to Mother Agnès on 7 July 1897. The latter had asked her to tell her again of what had happened after her offering to Love. And Thérèse replied with humour: *Mother, I told you the same day; but you did not pay any attention (Her Last Conversations).* And here are Thérèse's own words, it is likely that the event happened in June 1895:

> *Well, I was beginning the Way of the Cross, and all of a sudden, I was seized with such a violent love for God that I cannot explain it except by saying that it was as if I had been totally plunged into fire. Oh! what fire and what sweetness at one and the same time! I was burning with love and I felt that one moment, one second longer, and I could not have supported its ardour without dying. I understood then what the saints said about these states that they had experienced so often. I experienced it only once, and only for an instant, then I fell back into my usual state of dryness* (LC 7.7.2).

In a flash, Thérèse had been in contact with heaven, that is to say with God's glory or the fire of the burning bush. She understood that this fire was infinitely desirable but at the same time formidable because a person cannot see God and live (Ex 33:20). She felt this presence of God around her as the Jews had felt the presence of God's glory, under the form of a cloud by day and as a pillar of fire by night. This experience is alluring, but at the same time produces fear for it puts a person in contact with the 'high tension' of God's glory. Thérèse expressed it in this way: *It was as if I had been totally plunged into fire* (LC ibid).

Yet at the same time, this fire was all sweetness: *Oh! what fire and what sweetness at the same time* (LC ibid). Thérèse was to say. We need to understand the nature of this fire of God which is in itself strength and gentleness. In the world of the things of God, contraries are joined together when they are pushed to their paroxysm. The suffering of Christ on the cross was the abyss of dereliction, but at the same time it was also an abyss of glory and therefore of joy. We have only to look at Vladimir's Virgin of Tenderness to understand that in Mary, it is Calvary and Thabor at the same time, Good Friday and Easter Sunday. Teresa of Avila recalling this experience, said: 'The divine fire is an oil'. It is the unction of the Holy Spirit and therefore of God's gentleness: 'There seemed to be a fire in my soul, but this fire did not reach the centre; it seemed like an oil!' (St Teresa of Avila).

If we wish to understand Thérèse, we must ponder this mystery of God who is strength and gentleness. God is formidable like fire when he comes up against the hardness of a human heart, then he wishes to destroy the old heart with its marble carapace. But in the case of Thérèse who offers him no resistance, he is mercy and gentleness. She herself will say, using the symbolism of water, that after the act of offering, she had been invaded by waves of grace which came to flood her soul (Ms A 181).

In his book, *Il y a un autre monde*, André Frossard brings us to grips with this mystery: 'I learnt,' he writes, 'that he (God) is gentle, with a gentleness beyond compare, and this is not the passive quality that is sometimes meant by this word, but an active, shattering gentleness, surpassing all violence, capable of smashing the hardest rock, and harder than rock, the human heart.

Here we are faced with a veritable paradox. When God's glory begins to besiege our heart: either this glory appears as the fire from heaven which confronted the Israelites at Horeb: *Go down and warn the people not to cross the boundary to see the Lord coming, for many of them will perish* (Ex 19:21), or which destroyed the prophets of Baal on Mount Carmel

(1 Kings 18); or else we are not aware of it and pass by God's gentleness, like the Jews who did not know how to discern, in Jesus' humility and gentleness, the incarnation of the Son of God: *Is this not the carpenter's son?* (Mt 13:53).

'It is not the omnipotence of God that confronts us, continues André Frossard, nor what is called his Glory, from a word which has lost its true meaning and been dulled with decorative emphasis and devastating attributes. What is to be feared, is his gentleness. What his charity conceals from our sight is the nuclear fulguration of the Infinite One who shrinks in unimaginable humility. What breaks our hearts is God's eternal and limpid innocence. He cannot appear without our passing immediate sentence and final judgement on ourselves without remission. And this he cannot do. He covers everything with charity.

Before ... 'It was not real fire'

What happened in Thérèse's life after her act of offering to Love? To grasp this we must distinguish three moments: before, during and after. And do not think that here we are borrowing a scholastic definition or linguistic device, for Thérèse herself took care to distinguish these stages. After she described what happened during the Way of the Cross, she adds:

> From the age of fourteen years, I have known transports of love. Ah! how I loved God! but it was not at all LIKE THAT AFTER (we have emphasised these words) my offering to Love, it was not real fire that used to burn me (LC 7:7.2).

Of course, those who have not known the folly of merciful Love take these expressions to be imagery or metaphors. They attribute them to a very keen affectivity and find them more to be admired than imitated. They do not understand that the fire of God's love is more real and more burning than all the fires of this earth. But those who have had some experience of God, however small it might be, like St Paul, Claudel or Frossard, will understand instinctively what Thérèse is saying. St Augustine — another great convert — said: 'Give me a heart that loves and it will understand what I am saying.'

From the age of 14 years, Thérèse had known *assaults of love*, which comes back to saying that the love of the Trinity was flowing in her and that at certain moments it would spring up with great force. But after the act of offering, grace became glory in her, that is to say that the love of the Trinity had been brought to a degree of incandescence in her where it had become luminous and burning, capable of transforming her life. In her, the pillar of cloud became a pillar of fire.

Dostoïevsky said: 'My whole idea consists in red-hot burning inspiration'. Thérèse said: before *it was not real fire that was burning me* (ibid). So in her, sanctity is the red-hot burning of what is the basis of the whole Christian life, namely, the love of the Trinity: *I was burning with love and felt that another moment, another second longer, and I could not have supported its ardour without dying* (ibid).

Listening to these words, we feel that there is another death besides natural death and it is the death of love many of the saints have known. It is dying in prayer. Gregory of Nyssa relating the life of St Macrina, his sister, states that she died making 'thanksgiving': 'When she had finished her thanksgiving after Communion and indicated, by bringing her hand up to her face to make the sign of the cross, that she had finished her prayer, she gave a long, deep sigh and ceased at the same time her prayer and her life' (Gregory of Nyssa, *Life of Macrina*).

Thérèse clearly says that she understood then what the saints are saying about these states, but she added immediately:

For me, I experienced it only once and only for a single moment, then I fell back into my usual state of dryness. God has too much respect for men and women to make them live in this state of high tension which cannot be supported without damaging natural life. So God proceeds with delicate and strong touches to let us feel the violence of his love. And then, we have to understand the nature of this experience which changes a person profoundly and to their roots. Too often today we forget that such an experience leaves traces and that responsibility has to be taken for the results of it. You do not throw the waste into the dustbin as in a laboratory. It is the same for the less intense experiences, for example the weeks of prayer, the schools of prayer that can be seen flourishing today. Some people increase the number without suspecting that they are living more along the lines of consumption rather than of assimilation.

What happens then? Let us look at things concretely and compare Thérèse to the average Christian such as we are. Between us and Thérèse, there is only a difference of degree separating the dim glow and the luminous glow, at the exact moment when the body catches fire, when the solids liquify: 'The hearts of the saints are liquid', said the Curé of Ars. I was thinking about this very much when we were celebrating the centenary of Thérèse's birth. When she was baptised, 4 January 1873, in the church of Our Lady at Alençon, her beginning was the same as ours. You could say that the same life of the Trinity flowed through her veins, if we are not afraid of using a rather materialistic comparison.

But the difference appears at the moment when Thérèse will internalise this love of the Trinity during her childhood and adolescent years so that it will attain its highest point the moment she offers herself to merciful Love, on 9 June 1895. So the difference between Thérèse and us is not a difference of nature − it is the same life which circulates in her and in us − but a difference of intensity. With her, the Holy Spirit irrupting from without, through the sacraments of the Church and prayer, will light the brazier of Trinitarian love and bring it to such a degree of incandescence that it will consume her whole being. This is why we must now pause at that crucial moment when she is going to offer herself to merciful Love; after having looked at 'the after', we returned to 'the before'. It now remains for us to examine 'the during'.

'O my God! is your disdained love to remain within your heart?'

If it were possible to take a spiritual radioscopy of Thérèse's heart on the evening of 9 June 1895, what would we see there? A young 22-year-old girl in whom there was an extraordinary humility and a desire to love God still more. But then she discovers that her desire to love God is ridiculous when faced with God's exorbitant love for humanity. In other words, she sees God bending down over each one of his creatures, offering to share with them his infinite love, that is, the friendship of the Trinity, the secret that he shares with his Son. God begs for our response. Let us not forget that Thérèse made her discovery on Trinity Sunday, 9 June 1985!

It is a devouring love which desires the other with all the strength of its being but which is at the same time infinitely respectful of the person. If God's love is devouring, it devours first and foremost the one who loves and not the one who is loved. Here Thérèse is at one with the Eastern Fathers (I am thinking also of Nicholas Cabasilas) for whom God is the beggar of love who knocks at the door of our heart (Rev 3:20). She does not think first about loving God but rather of understanding the depth of his love for her.

Let us note in passing the two characteristics of the climate of this offering. Firstly its Trinitarian character: it is a love which comes from the Trinity and which returns to it. Then, its sacramental character. Thérèse does not 'soar up' directly into the mystery of the Holy Trinity, she knows that she has to pass through Christ and therefore through the Church in order to be united with the Trinity. She understands exactly where this love is coming from and where it is going. As Cardinal Ratzinger said so well, each time we approach Christ, we must pose a twofold question: 'From whence does he come and where is he going?' If we neglect to situate him in this way, we are cutting Christ off from his source and making him a 'humanist'. And if we neglect his intent, that is to say the salvation he brings to humanity, we are making a false 'spiritualism' from the Gospel.

I have always been struck by the tragic character of Thérèse's words when she speaks of the love of God that wants to give itself to men and women and which is disdained by them. Listen to these words in the silence of prayer:

O my God, I cried from the depths of my heart, is it only your justice which will receive souls willing to offer themselves as victims? … Does not your merciful Love need them also? … On all sides this love is unknown, rejected; those hearts upon whom you would pour it out turn to creatures seeking their happiness from them with their miserable affection instead of throwing themselves into your arms and accepting your infinite Love (Ms A 180).

If we dare to speak like Fr Varillon in his wonderful book, *La Souffrance de Dieu*, we would say that God suffers, not because he is frustrated by something, but because of the fullness of the love which he is not able to pour out. When we begin to consider God's love from this angle, it is no longer a question of us offering our poor human love, but of convincing our head that we can, by offering our poverty and our misery, so that God can fill it completely. God alone is capable of filling the human heart with a superabundance of merciful Love. Let us not forget that when we are confronted by another's misery, we do not need to have a mercy 'complex', only the living God in us can be merciful and fill the emptiness of our brothers and sisters.

Let us listen to Thérèse again:

O my God; Is your merciful Love to remain within your heart? It seems to me that if you were to find souls offering themselves as victims of holocaust to your Love, you would rapidly consume them (one thinks here of the flame which devoured her during the Way of the Cross), it seems to me that you would be happy not to hold back the waves of infinite tenderness within you ... If your justice likes to release itself, which extends only on earth, how much more does your merciful Love desire to set souls afire since your mercy reaches to the heavens (Ms A 181).

With regard to this act of offering to Love, it must be noted that Thérèse is standing out in marked contrast with those around her where there was the custom of offering oneself to God's justice. It would be thought that she would fall into step and follow her sisters. Not at all! Thérèse in speaking of this act of offering to justice says: *But I was far from feeling myself drawn to make it* (Ms A 180). This requires a very high degree of maturity since she is breaking with the customs of her milieu in order to affirm her own vocation which is to offer herself to Love.

'Jesus! that I might be that happy victim ...'

When Jesus said: '*I have come to bring fire to the earth and how I wish it were blazing already* (Lk 12:49), he is showing us quite simply what he has contemplated in the Father's heart, that is, God's infinite love for humanity. According to John's word, Jesus is the Father's 'exegete' (Jn 1:18). He came to make known to us the earnest desire of his Father who is searching for adorers in spirit and truth with whom he can share his tenderness. It is another way of saying: 'O my God, is your disdained Love to remain within your heart?'

Jesus is the one who has 'humanised' in his body the fire of the burning bush and has put it within our reach in the Eucharist, so that we might be able to receive it in our 'vessels of clay' which are our poor human bodies. This is the very meaning of Thérèse's offering; she offered to God her humanity in order to receive the waves of infinite tenderness closed up within the heart of God: *O my Jesus! That I might be that happy victim, consume your holocaust through the fire of your divine Love* (Ms A 181).

It comes back to a person offering himself or herself to God and this is the mystery of oblation. But there is another aspect of holocaust such as Thérèse of Lisieux understood it. In the mystery of holocaust, the fire of the burning bush supervenes from outside and makes the Trinitarian life red-hot. It brings it to a state of high incandescence. God is a devouring, consuming fire, and he transforms into himself all that he touches.

It is also important to note that Thérèse's mysticism is lived in an ecclesial and sacramental context. It is in and through the Eucharist that she offers herself to merciful Love: 'On Sunday, 9 June 1895 — on the feast of the Holy Trinity — during Mass, she was inspired to offer herself as a victim of holocaust to the merciful Love of God in order to receive, in her heart, all the love disdained by the creatures on whom he wished to lavish it' (CSG).

When he invited Christians to draw near the body of Christ, St John Chrysostom used to say: 'You are going to commune with fire!' Beyond these words of Thérèse, influenced by her epoch, it is good to see that she joins, in the act of offering, the whole Eastern tradition in which the Eucharist is linked to the fire of the burning bush. For evidence, I will quote St Simeon Metaphrastis' prayer which he composed for Christians before Communion.

'Trembling, I hope in you. I am communing with fire. Of myself, I am but straw, but, O miracle, I feel myself suddenly blazing like Moses' burning bush of old. Lord, your whole body shines with the fire of your divinity, ineffably united with it. And you grant me that the corruptible temple of my flesh be united with your holy flesh, that my blood is mixed with yours and henceforth I am your transparent and luminous member.

'You have given me your flesh as food. You who are a fire which consumes the unworthy, do not burn me, O my Creator, but rather slip into my members, into all my joints, into my loins and into my heart. Consume the thorns of all my sins, purify my soul, sanctify my heart, strengthen the tendons of my knees and my bones, illumine my five senses and establish me wholly in your love.'

The living flame becomes living water

The act of offering to Love is situated here:

> In order to live in one act of perfect love, I am offering myself as a victim of holocaust to your merciful Love, begging you to consume me unceasingly, allowing the waves of infinite tenderness shut up within you to overflow into my soul ... (Clarke 276).

It is a question here of merciful Love which fills up human nothingness by consuming the person, without the latter ceasing to be weak.

As St John of the Cross states, the Living Flame burns and destroys all obstacles. But, according to another Scriptural image symbolising the Holy Spirit, the Living Flame becomes Living Water as soon as it no longer meets with any obstacle. It is the mystery of God's gentleness we referred to when speaking of the event which took place during the Way of the Cross (14 June 1895). Instead of burning, this living water refreshes, calms and pacifies. It is the total peace of one engulfed completely in the trinitine glory.

And this brings us back to conclude with what happened after the act of offering. There is indeed the event of the Way of the Cross, but there is also the state of soul Thérèse described in these words:

Dearest Mother, you gave me permission to offer myself in this way to God, you know the waves (again the living Water) *or rather the oceans of grace which have come to inundate my soul ... Ah! since that happy day, it seems to me that Love penetrates and surrounds me at each moment, this merciful Love is renewing me, purifying my soul and not leaving there any trace of sin* (Ms 181).

Thérèse will never regret having surrendered herself to Love (these were her last words); on the contrary she will invite all her friends to enter into this offering to merciful Love, but she immediately makes very clear that this offering demands that one live in confidence and abandonment: *Oh! How sweet is the way of Love! How I want to apply myself to doing God's will always with greater self-surrender* (Ms A 181).

Confidence and nothing but confidence! It is the only way that leads to Love. These words of Thérèse sum up the whole of her manuscript. We will return to this in the next chapter but let us not wait until then to offer ourselves to Love. You who are reading these lines, stop. Silence all the thoughts running around in your head and offer your nothingness to this Love who does not cease asking for it. This supposes that you have no other desire but God and his love: 'Lord,' prayed Teihard de Chardin, 'my desire for you is a sort of fire'. And he continued in his letter to a friend: 'Pray that under no circumstances, I allow myself to want anything else but the fire.'

5

'Confidence and nothing but confidence'

Thérèse's inspired intuition had been to discover and to understand the deepest and most mysterious face of God, that of his mercy which Jesus came on earth to reveal to us. Then she no longer had any hesitation, she surrendered herself without reserve and God invaded her with his merciful Love. This is what we have tried to say in our preceding chapter. But Thérèse knew that few would understand this face: *He* (Jesus) finds, alas! few souls who surrender themselves to him unreservedly, who understand all the tenderness of his infinite Love (LT 196).

But there is still more about Thérèse, and that is what makes her an *adorer in spirit and in truth, such as the Father seeks* (Jn 4:23). She has not only discovered this face of mercy, but she has sung this testimony with joy and exultation for she has the charism of the Magnificat. And I am struck when reading the manuscripts how many times this word is repeated again and again by Thérèse's pen, not only at the beginning, but also at the end. As in manuscript 'C', she wrote to Mother Marie de Gonzague: *You wanted me to sing with you the mercies of the Lord.*

And to sing in this way, something other than testimony is needed, love is needed. In other words, there must be total self-forgetfulness and God-centredness. If we have so much

67

difficulty praying, praising God and adoring him, it is not so much due to the exterior circumstances of our life (lack of time, mental dissipation, activity) as to our stony heart, hard and shrivelled up in itself. This is the 'natura curva' of which St Bernard speaks concerning the cure of the woman who was bent over in the Gospel, 'she was incapable of looking at heaven' (Lk 13:10), that is to pray and to chant the mercies of the Lord.

Thérèse blesses God, that is she turns her face towards the Face of God to adore him and in this way she fulfils the true nature of every man and woman which is adoration and praise. It is the desire to praise God which compels her to offer herself to merciful Love. Love compels her to go right to the end of this overture to the joy of God.

The oblation is the utterance of Thérèse's sacrifice, but there is another thing in her offering, for she surrenders herself to merciful Love as a victim of holocaust. It is God's response, the fire from heaven which comes to consume the victim. Oblatory love compels her to offer herself, but she does not truly become a victim before she is consumed by the fire of the burning bush. Thérèse explains it in this way in manuscript 'B'. Let us note in passing the last sentence which alludes to merciful Love, that is, to God's love bending down over human nothingness and misery:

> *I am only a child, powerless and weak, and yet my very weakness gives me the boldness to offer myself as a victim of your Love, O Jesus! In past times only pure and spotless victims would be accepted by the strong and powerful God. Victims had to be perfect in order to satisfy divine justice, but the law of fear has given way to the law of Love, and Love has chosen me as a holocaust, me, a weak and imperfect creature ... Is not this choice worthy of Love? Yes, in order that love might be fully satisfied, it must humble itself, humble itself to nothingness and transform that nothingness into fire* (Ms B 195).

'It must humble itself to nothingness ...'

It is here that we must take into account the heavy expenditure, if we wish to follow Thérèse in her act of offering to Love. It is not a question of *climbing the rough stairway of fear but of being raised up to God by the lift of love* (LT 258). Thérèse is not speaking here of the love that our generosity produces or our will exercises, but a love which comes down from above, from the heart of the Three and is engulfed in our nothingness. If this nothingness is not discovered, opened out and offered to God love cannot fill it.

And it is there that we join Sr Marie of the Sacred Heart, Thérèse's sister. When Thérèse was on retreat, in September 1896, and she realised her vocation: *In the heart of the Church, my Mother, I will be Love; in this way I will be everything.* Her sister Marie had asked her the secret of her way of childhood. And Thérèse had replied with the first part of manuscript 'B'. She had let herself go and sang of her desires for martyrdom and for all vocations on the gamut of ultra-sound as Fr Molinié says, in a flight which is, as well as being extraordinary, one of the summits of spiritual literature:

Martyrdom, that was the dream of my youth ... and it still is, yet I feel that my dream is folly for I know that I cannot limit my desires to one kind of martyrdom. I would have to have them all to satisfy me ...' There follows the description of all the kinds of martyrdom ... St Bartholomew, St John, St Agnes, St Cecila ... *Jesus, Jesus, if I wanted to write down all my desires, I would have to borrow your book of life.*

When Marie received Thérèse's letter she found it more to be admired than to be imitated. Faced with the sight of such fire, she says to her sister: 'You are indeed possessed by God's love as others are possessed by the devil!' She felt that her sister's great desires were far removed from the encouraging prospects of the little way. And she ventured to say: 'It is all very beautiful, but it is not for me'. This shows a lack of faith and of hope. With her usual inspired finesse, Thérèse realised that she had made a mistake in letting herself go and sing her desires in the ultrasonic scale. Her sister's ears were not yet attuned to hear this melody.

Thérèse quickly hastens to put things right with a forcible restatement which is no less remarkable and intrepid in its charity than her desires for martyrdom in their folly. Let us note that Thérèse begins her letter with her sister's own words to her: 'You are possessed by God's love as one is possessed by the devil!' Then Thérèse replies:

> *How can you ask me if it is possible for you to love God as I love him? If you had understood the story of the little bird, you would not be asking this question. My desires for martyrdom are nothing, the boundless confidence I feel in my heart does not come from them. In fact they are the spiritual riches which make us unjust when we rest in them complacently and think we are something great (...)*
>
> *How can you say after that that my desires are a mark of my love? Ah! I know that this is not what pleases God in my little soul. What does please him, is the blind hope I have in his mercy ... That is my only treasure, dearest Godmother, why should this treasure not be yours?* (17 September, 1896).

'To love my littleness and my poverty ...'

Without despising her desires — Thérèse knows only too well that they come from the Holy Spirit — she regards them as riches which makes us unjust if we put our confidence in them: *What pleases God, is to see me love my littleness and my poverty.* It is not only a question of discovering and ascertaining her nothingness, it is necessary that she also love it and rejoice in it. To understand this better, let us call on another sister of Thérèse, Céline, who had entered Carmel in 1894 and who, as we have seen, had brought with her a note-book in which she had copied out words from Scripture on the way of childhood.

While having understood it intellectually, Céline had great difficulty in accepting it effectively and acknowledging her poverty. At Les Buissonnets, Thérèse and Céline had been very united (the conversations in the Belvedere were likened to those between Monica and Augustine). When she entered Carmel, Céline is dumbfounded to see her sister up with the 'shooting stars' while she is still crawling along the plain. Then she goes and complains to her sister and compares herself with her: 'How I would like to offer God your tactfulness!' she said, and Thérèse answered her: *Thank God that you are without tact*.

Thérèse suggested to her sister Céline that she unite herself to God starting with her poverty and the latter refused. So when she said to her one day: 'When I think of all that I have to acquire,' Thérèse replied: *Say rather to lose! Jesus will fill your soul with splendour to the degree that you rid it of its imperfections*. It is indeed the blade of the guillotine which falls to cut Céline's last illusions. Little Placid comes to mind here when he complained and received the reply: 'You are not yet shorn enough!' Thérèse tried to make her sister understand that God was not attracted to her because of her virtues or her riches, but because of her poverty, and I would say, her 'unsanctity'. We are always too rich and too loaded up to pass through the narrow gate. And as we have said before, we always envisage perfection as a going-up when it is a descent in humility: '*Whoever exalts himself will be humbled, whoever humbles himself will be exalted.*

When we try to raise ourselves up, to grow up, we infallibly cut the subtle and sweet communication between Love and non-love, between being and nothing. We will not be united to God by likeness, but by distinction, that is to say by offering him our poverty. The only prayer that will touch the Father's heart, is that of the publican in the Gospel: 'Lord, be merciful to me!' Again Thérèse says to Céline: *You will never reach perfection if you insist on climbing a mountain and God wants to make you go down into the fertile valley where you will learn to despise yourself* (CSG).

The gift of knowledge enables us to experience our nothingness as a creature before the sanctity of God. In the spiritual life, to love one's weakness with sweetness is an art! Thérèse explains it in this way to her sister Céline:

> *I also have my weaknesses, but I rejoice in them. I do not always succeed either in rising above the trifles of this earth, for example, I will be tormented by some silly thing I have said or done! Then I reflect and say to myself: 'Alas! I am still at the same place as I was before!' But I tell myself this with great gentleness and without sadness. It is so good to feel oneself weak and little* (LC 5:7.1).

Here we are at the heart of Theresian spirituality. When merciful Love teaches us these things, we not only discover the truth of the nothingness of the creature but also the charm of this poverty and we begin to appreciate and savour how good it is to be nothing: *It is so good to feel oneself weak and little* (ibid). 'You create the capacity and I will make myself a torrent.' The hollow in us is the capacity to be invaded by the torrent of Trinitarian love.

It is traditional language in the Church and especially with St Paul. Thérèse refers to the second letter to the Corinthians (12:7-10) and speaks of 'the science that teaches us to glory in our infirmities'. She adds that it is a great grace to discover this. And here, she joins the great current of Eastern spirituality. Did not St Isaac the Syrian say: 'The one who weeps over his sins is greater than the one who sees God or who raises to life a dead person.' Let us listen again to Thérèse speaking to her cousin:

> You are mistaken if you think that your little Thérèse always walks with fervour along the road of virtue. She is weak, very weak. Every day she makes some new discovery of it. But Jesus is pleased to teach her, like St Paul, the science of glorying in her infirmities. This is indeed a great grace, and I ask Jesus to teach it to you for it is only in this that the heart finds its peace and rest. When we see ourselves so miserable, we no longer want to look at ourselves and we look only at the sole Beloved (LT 109).

The truly poor in spirit ... where is he?'

Here we are also at the heart of the gospel message of the Beatitudes: *Blessed are the poor in spirit for theirs is the kingdom of heaven*. It is also to be found in the Gospel: humility, poverty, gentleness and the spirit of childhood. Few are prepared to take up their misery as if it were a precious pearl, difficult to find and worthy of enthusiastic searching. Our natural tendency is to run away from this misery or to make excuses for it. This flight does not imply however the desire to free ourselves from it, but an obscure and grim refusal to acknowledge it and to be confronted by such a sight.

Following all the saints, Thérèse puts before us, by making us experience it, the tenderness with which Jesus regards and loves our misery. He suffered much more from it than we do because he alone is human. He is the only one who has a heart of flesh, our hearts are made of stone. Thérèse invites us to accept this misery, not in a merciless clearsighted way, but with a deeper clearsightedness which teaches us how to discover, through the action of the Spirit, that this poverty is the perfect weapon which gives us absolute power over the merciful heart of God.

73

Jesus came for the poor, the sick and sinners, in other words, for all those 'who are not well in their skin'. If we rank ourselves among the just, the rich or the 'well' people, we no longer need his mercy for our sanctity depends on our own sheer strength of arm.

God desires to find lowly hearts: 'The weaker one is,' says Thérèse, 'the more fit he or she is for the operations of consuming Love.' He is ready to give us all the gifts he gave Thérèse and all the saints, provided that we offer him, as she did, our misery. He loves us as beings to be filled and this is why Thérèse loved her misery and opened it out humbly before God. She understood that it is at this depth that God made an appointment with her and he is waiting for her. It is there and only there that his mercy is hidden.

It is in this sense that Thérèse says firmly that it is necessary to go very far and very deep to find one who is poor in spirit and who is not with the great souls but in nothingness. We never go down deeply enough into our misery to cry to God. A prayer that comes from the depths is always heard. We understand also that this nothingness can be a source of despair if we look at it from a debilitating human viewpoint, but it is a source of tremendous hope if we look at it with the eyes of mercy:

> Understand that to love Jesus, to be his victim of love, the weaker one is, without desires or virtue, the more ready one is for the operations of that consuming and transforming love. The very desire to be a victim suffices, but one must consent to remain always poor and without strength, and this is the difficulty, for 'where are we to find one who is truly poor in spirit? He must be sought afar', says the psalmist. He does not say that we must look for him among the great souls, but 'afar', that is in lowliness, in nothingness. Ah! let us keep far away from all that shines, let us love our littleness, let us love to feel nothing, then we will be poor in spirit and

*Jesus will come for us, far off as we are, and transform us
into a flame of love ... Oh! how I wish I could make you
understand what I feel! ... It is confidence and nothing but
confidence that must bring us to Love* (LT 197).

'Jesus is offended by the lack of confidence'

In the spiritual life, there is only one thing to fear: lack of
confidence in God. We grieve so often over our weaknesses
which humiliate us. Thérèse understood so well that there
are weaknesses which do not offend God, but make him
smile. These miseries are for God's mercy as grain is for the
mill: *It seems to me that Jesus can give the grace of no longer
offending him or committing faults that do not offend him but
only serve to humble and strengthen love* (LT 114).

A great saint of the east, Isaac the Syrian, said: 'There
is only one sin and that is not to believe in the Risen Christ.
All the other sins are nothing, for God gives us repentance
to atone for them.' Thérèse was to say practically the same
thing: *What offends Jesus and wounds his heart is the lack of
confidence* (LT 92).

Do we want to know how much confidence we have? Let
us ask ourselves the question: 'If one morning, we wake up
and our heart is weighed down with every possible sin, would
we have enough confidence to go and throw ourselves at
Jesus' feet and humbly ask his forgiveness?'

*Yes, I feel it; even though I had on my conscience every sin
that can be committed, I would go, my heart broken with
sorrow, and throw myself into Jesus' arms, because I know
how much he loves the prodigal who returns to him. It is not
because God, in his prevenient mercy, has preserved my soul
from mortal sin that I go to him with confidence and love
...* (Ms C 259).

75

*If I had committed every possible crime, I would still have
the same confidence. I feel that this whole multitude of offences
would be as a drop of water thrown into a blazing furnace*
(LC 11.7.6).

'It is confidence and nothing but confidence ...'

The whole of St Thérèse's writing can be summed up in
this last word: *It is confidence and nothing but confidence that
must bring us to Love* (LT 197). It is already very formidable!
Usually, we try to go to God, to search for him and to love
him through confidence and also through something else.
We search for supports, signs, securities in our merits, our
qualities and our milieu. The characteristic quality of confidence is to rely on nothing else but love and mercy. While
we search for God through some means other than confidence alone, we cease to have him as our one support. Some
days, instead of making acts of confidence, we make so many
acts of non-confidence, of non-love: 'My God, I do not have
enough confidence in you. Increase my faith and my love!'

The one who has confidence resembles the Blessed Virgin.
She did not understand (Lk 1:34), but she knew that 'nothing
is impossible with God' (Lk 1:37). Then she did not look
at herself any more at all, in order to fix her gaze solely on
God alone. She belongs truly with that great gallery of witnesses to the faith that Paul depicts in chapters 11 and 12
of the letter to the Hebrews. They leave their own country
and set off for an unknown land, because their eyes were
always fixed on Jesus the witness to the faith (Heb 12:2).
The Word of God is their only compass.

The Blessed Virgin could have had 'evidence' that all
the human outlets were closed or blocked, but she had a

continuous preference for the 'evidence' of God who is Master of the impossible. She had that inexplicable suppleness of one who prefers God's thought to his or her own. This was why she was able to go forward along a road that was humanly blocked; *Everything is possible for one who believes*, Jesus said, to the father of the possessed child (Mk 9:23).

This is Thérèse's definition for confidence and abandonment: to be totally forgetful of self so as to be centred on God: *When we see ourselves so miserable*, she says, *we no longer want to look at ourselves and we look only at the sole Beloved* (LT 109).

So our confidence must give up all its human supports so that we might be rooted in Jesus our only rock. All the spiritual impurities come because we are relying on something else. And this is why the Holy Spirit takes away from us one by one our human supports and our securities in order to teach us true confidence.

Instinctively, we depend or rely on what we see or feel, so God sets about teaching us the science of the 'Nothing'. No longer having anything on which to anchor ourselves, we are obliged to take the plunge into God alone.

This doctrine of confidence is important above all for our search for God. We want to prove to him our love and then we make, like St Paul, resolutions prompted by generosity. We promise God that we will give him our life. Without knowing it, we are giving a lever to Satan who is going to sift us (Lk 22:31), for we are still counting too much on our own strength. When Jesus said to Peter: *I have prayed that your faith might not fail*, this is precisely what he wanted to make us understand: do not make promises based only on generosity alone. The day we understand this, we will discover the science and the power of prayer and instead of making resolutions, we will transform them into prayer:

Instead of saying: 'My God, I am going to do this', we say: 'My God, teach me to do this!'

On this subject, Thérèse said:

If, instead of saying, 'I will give my life for you', poor St Peter had said to Christ: 'You know only too well that I am incapable of giving my life for you, come to my aid', he would have surely overcome that temptation. Like Thérèse, we should be able to say: *It is confidence and nothing but confidence that must bring us to Love.*

We discover here the importance of the prayer of supplication which is linked to humility and confidence. By ourselves, we can do nothing, then our only chance of salvation is to cry to God and to beseech him: 'Have mercy on us, come to our aid!' Those who understand Thérèse's word cry for help and by their supplication they are engulfed in continual prayer. It is often a leap in despair that thrusts us into blind confidence and into real prayer.

This is why Thérèse said: *How necessary it is to pray for the dying! If you only knew!* Essentially the dying are in the truth, they can no longer rely on anything else but mercy. Another great saint, Francis Xavier who very nearly died when he was crossing from India to Japan, wrote to his brothers from Goa: 'My brothers, what will the hour of our death be for us, if, during our life, we have not prepared ourselves and disposed ourselves to the science of hope and confidence in God? For, at that moment, we find ourselves in greater temptations, sufferings and trials than ever before, in mind as well as body. This is why those who wish to live with the desire of serving God must work to humble themselves very much in little things, to be diffident, to establish themselves and be deeply grounded in God. For, as we know so well: in the great dangers and trials, during life and at the hour of death, we will be able to place our hope in the sovereign goodness and mercy of God, in the measure that we have exerted ourselves to overcome temptations and repugnances, however small they might be, mistrusting self in all humility, and fortifying the heart through great confidence in God. No one is weak when he makes good use of the grace which Our Lord gives him' (S. Francis Xavier, *Spiritual Letters*, edited by Fr Brou, Spes 1937). All the saints agree when it comes to confidence or, according to Xavier's expression, 'the science of hope and confidence in God'.

'Everything is decided for us,' says Fr Molinié, 'in the play between mercy and confidence. There are no other problems, difficulties, mistakes in our life. I say: absolutely no others'. Like Thérèse, we have to learn to practise love or, which is the same thing, to practise confidence. There is nothing more simple than to trust since it is a question of abandoning oneself to God like a child (to have confidence is as easy as breathing), but it is at the same time very complicated and difficult because we are so little used to it. We lack the flexibility to continually opt for God's thought in preference to our own.

We realise all too well how far we are from 'raising ourselves up to God by the lift of love and not climbing the rough stairway of fear'. But can we take to ourselves the promise she made to Abbé Bellière some months before her death, she who had promised to *spend* (her) heaven doing good on earth:

> I am not surprised at all that the practice of familiarity with Jesus seems a little difficult for you to achieve. You cannot come to it in a day, but I am sure that I will help you much better to walk this delightful way when I am free of my mortal envelope and, soon, like St Augustine, you will say: 'Love is the weight that draws me' (LT 258).

II

'Now, abandonment alone guides me'

6

Thérèse discovers the road of abandonment

We have closely examined Christianity's most profound mystery, that of mercy, to know that Jesus *came to call not the just but sinners* (Mt 9:13). Thérèse understood in a wonderful way that God was expecting from her faith in mercy and not in sacrifice. And throughout the *Manuscripts*, she will sing only the mercies of the Lord in her regard.

But it must never be forgotten that if God's love is gratuitous, that is to say that we can never pay him back in return with his own currency, it is nevertheless arbitrary. There is something in us that can draw the heart of God and that we alone can give him. God is waiting for us to give him that which only a human being has the power to give: humility and confidence. This is why the last chapter ended with Thérèse's word: *It is confidence and nothing but confidence that must bring us to Love* (LT 197).

How did Thérèse live out this confidence and this humility, day by day, in a concrete attitude that we will call Abandonment? She herself will say to Mother Agnès of Jesus, at the end of manuscript A: *Abandonment alone guides me, I have no other compass ...! I can no longer pray for anything with fervour, except the perfect fulfilment of God's will in my soul without any creatures being able to prevent it* (Ms A 178).

The word 'abandonment' in itself is not without ambiguity and it will probably make us change, so this is why we will have to give it x-ray treatment, in order to restore to it the active character Christ gave it in the Gospel and which has been understood in the whole spiritual tradition. We prefer the expression used by Fr Victor Sion[1] when he speaks of the 'movement of abandonment'. It is indeed a question of a movement which is passive and active at the same time since we receive from God the impetus of his love, and we invest our intelligence, our will and our affectivity so that in the end we surrender unreservedly to this love.

To receive is no less active than to do or to take, but it is an activity of another order which, in the eyes of human impatience, unfortunately resembles passivity. Thérèse always maintained and taught the novices that her way of spiritual childhood had nothing in common with quietism, but it must be clearly understood what part the individual has to play in this. Her sister Céline expressed it in these words:

> 'Although she walked by this way of blind and complete confidence which she called her 'little way', or 'way of spiritual childhood', she never minimised personal co-operation. Her whole life of generous and sustained acts shows the importance she attached to it' (CSG).

But for the moment, we wish to leave aside this aspect of 'personal co-operation', to which we will return later, in order to show how much Theresian abandonment is rooted in the Gospel and in spiritual tradition. Studying the different 'schools of spirituality', we have been struck by the fact that on this precise point of abandonment they are all in agreement. This is of course normal, since every particular spirituality has its source in the Gospel and, in the beginning,

1 *'Spiritual Realism of St Thérèse of Lisieux'*, Victor Sion.

84

there is a fire event, a conversion, that is to say the over-whelming encounter with Christ. They stand in opposition when they become cold and when each takes advantage of 'its' spirituality to oppose that of the other, in the beginning there is fire. But there is a precise point where they do come together, and that is the moment where it is necessary to incarnate love of God's will into everyday living. For Eastern spirituality, it will be the control of the thoughts in the name of the Lord Jesus, for St John of the Cross, the anagogical or spiritual act, for Fr de Caussade, abandonment to Providence, for St Ignatius examination of conscience, for others, the present moment and for Thérèse, this way of abandonment.

This road is abandonment

Let us look at how Thérèse sees abandonment. She does not define it, but she lives it before our eyes. She speaks explicitly about the science of Love:

> My soul, she says, desires only this science ... I understand so clearly that only love can make us pleasing to God and this love is the only good I ardently desire. Jesus is pleased to show me the road that leads to this divine furnace, and this is the road of the surrender of the little child who sleeps without fear in its father's arms ... (Ms B 188).

Then follow two quotations from Scripture: Prov 9:4 and Wis 6:7, the second linked directly with mercy: The mercy shown to the little ones.

Jesus is the one who always teaches Thérèse interiorly and he shows her the way she must take. And exteriorly, Scripture comes to confirm this interior word. We have here a very important law of the spiritual life. As soon as we really pray with the heart, God must speak to us in our heart. Silouane of Athos, a great man of the spirit, wrote: 'When a soul is completely abandoned to God's will, the Lord himself begins to guide it, whereas formerly it had been guided by masters and by Scripture.'

And Christ can show Thérèse nothing else but what he had lived himself during his whole life, he, whose food was abandonment to the Father's will (Jn 4:33-34). Christ reveals here what was the fundamental law of his whole existence: *I do not seek my own will, but the will of the One who sent me.* Abandonment is nothing else but total surrender of our will to the Father's will. When Jesus came forth from the Father to come into this world, he made his own the words of Psalm 39, according to the author of the letter to the Hebrews:

> *Thus coming into this world, Christ said: You did not want sacrifice and offering, but you have prepared a body for me. Holocausts and sacrifices for sin are not pleasing to you. Then I said: Here am I, for as it is written of me in the scroll of the book; I come, O God, to do your will* (Heb 10:5-7).

Christ took his place in the long line of the great witnesses to the faith of which the letter to the Hebrews speaks, in chapters 11 and 12. All these men continually preferred God's thought to their own. The Blessed Virgin herself will say: *Here am I* for she had heard that *nothing is impossible to God.* Urs von Balthasar will say that Christ learnt from the Blessed Virgin to say this *yes* throughout his whole life. And this is what constitutes the real relationship of the disciples of Christ: *Whoever does the will of God, is my brother, my sister, my mother* (Mk 3:35). And when Christ will teach his disciples to pray, he will have them ask the Father: *Thy will be done on earth as it is in heaven.* Let us note in passing the passive form of this prayer: we ask God that his will be done and immediately abandon ourselves to that will.

It is significant that in the very passage where Thérèse says that Jesus has shown her the way of abandonment, she quotes another psalm where it is said that God has no need of our sacrifices but of our praise (Ps 49:9-13).

Jesus asks only abandonment

Ah! if all weak and imperfect souls felt what the least of all souls feels, the soul of your little Thérèse, not one would despair of reaching the summit of the mountain of love, since Jesus does not ask for great deeds, but only abandonment and gratitude ... This is all Jesus requires of us, he does not need our works, but only our love (Ms B 188).

The whole of Christ's life was a loving acceptance and complete abandonment to the Father's good pleasure. From the moment when Jesus heard at his Baptism his Father's word: *'You are my beloved Son, with you I am well pleased'*, until the moment when he said on the Cross: *Father into your hands I commend my spirit* (Lk 23:46), Jesus interiorised this love and lived it in one movement of abandonment.

In the life of Christ there is a moment when this abandonment will reach its climax and shine out before the eyes of the three apostles, and this is at the agony in the garden of Gethsemane. He prays that this chalice might pass from him, but adds immediately: *Not what I will, but as you will.* Christ knows well that the Father hears every prayer – he himself had taught this to his own (Mt 7:7) – but he also knew through experience that the Father answers our prayers in a way that is totally different from what we are expecting.

In the letter to the Hebrews (5:7), it is said that Jesus' prayer in the garden of Olives was heard because of his piety and that God raised him from the dead. But it is not a question of an immediate response from God who could have delivered him from his hour. God gave Christ the strength to accept, to consent and to abandon himself in order to

87

accomplish the work of salvation. In the same spirit we can ask the intercession of the saints: we make known to them our desires, but confide to them the task of asking them in accord with God's will, which they know so well.

This was how Thérèse acted 'when she expressed her desire *to do good upon earth*, she added this condition: *Before answering all those who will pray to me, I will begin by looking into the eyes of God to see if what I am asking for is not contrary to his will.* 'She made us note that this abandonment was in imitation of the prayer of the Blessed Virgin at Cana who was content to say: *They have no wine.* And as Martha and Mary said together: *The one whom you love is sick.* They simply put forward their desires, without formulating demands, leaving Jesus free to do his own will' (CSG).

We now return to the text at the beginning where Thérèse speaks of the road of abandonment that Jesus himself taught her and she states precisely why it is necessary to abandon oneself. The reason is simple: we are children in the arms of our father: *This road is the abandonment of the little child that sleeps in the arms of its father* (Ms B 188). When a child is in its father's arms, it does not need to be tense or strained, it can relax and surrender itself to the love of the one carrying it for it is experiencing his tenderness.

It is interesting that Thérèse goes instinctively to comparisons used in the Bible. When Hosea wanted to express the tenderness that the Lord had for Israel, he used the image of the father who carries his children in his arms:

When Israel was a child, I loved him ... I took them in my arms and they did not understand that I was taking care of them! I led them with the cords of compassion and bands of love; I was for them like one who lifts up an infant and presses it to the cheek, I bent down to them and fed them (Hos 11:4).

The child in its father's arms

Abandonment to the will of God would be a deception if God were not a Father attentive to his children's smallest desire. Re-read Luke 12:22-32 where Jesus says: *Do not be anxious about food or clothing ... The pagans of this world search for these things unceasingly, but you, your Father knows what you need.* When one understands that God is a Father who watches over each moment of our life and who counts each hair of our head, one can only abandon oneself to him and no longer be afraid. From the moment we let go and hand over our difficulties to the Father, we become free and we are at peace. If abandonment is necessary for us, it is quite simply because God is a Father who is tender and attentive to the needs of his children. Jesus abandoned himself to the Father because he was sure of his unfailing love.

When Jesus says this, he is telling us what he has seen in his Father who sees and knows our needs. Jesus reveals his Father's attentive gaze because he himself experiences the constant joy of living under this gaze: *You are my beloved Son.* And this conviction of being gazed on by an attentive and interested Father, is the faith Jesus asks for and recommends to his own. It is not an easy faith; because it is not evident and because God's silence is often more tangible than his attention. This is precisely the faith that demands enough confidence in God not to ask him for signs, that considers him great enough to dare to rely on his creature.

Thérèse, having tested spiritual childhood interiorly, will understand instinctively the way of abandonment. We will not conclude without citing all the texts where she refers to this divine paternity in the strict sense. She says of herself that she is a *child who is the object of a Father's provident love* (Ms A 84). She is *the child who looks on her Father's treasures* as her own (Ms A 140). She can give *the name of 'Father' to our Father who is in heaven* (Ms C 234).

The abandonment Thérèse lived is a component of her filial spirit. When her sisters will speak later of her little way of spiritual childhood, it is necessary to take care not to see it simply as moral behaviour or as a pious attitude that she adopted to be a nice person. For Thérèse, it is the very life of Christ or the soul of the Word. The Word was the first to have the spirit of childhood and has taught us abandonment. Or more precisely, the Word has the filial spirit, which is the first component of the spirit of childhood, says Fr Molinié, and the creature adds to it a nuance of littleness which shelters it.

In order to understand Theresian abandonment, it is necessary to believe that God begets us by adoption just as he begets his Word by nature and this is why the way of childhood is not a way 'on the cheap'. It is the very secret Christ came to reveal to his own. Basically, the reason Jesus came on earth was to communicate to us, by means of his Spirit, the experience of the Father that had been his for all eternity and to teach us abandonment.

Only the spirit of childhood can sound the depths of the Father, and we have to sound these depths and know the gifts God has given us (1 Cor 2:12). Thérèse says that every good thought belongs to the Holy Spirit and not to us *since St Paul says that without this Spirit of Love we are not able to give the name 'Father' to our Father in heaven* (Ms C 234). So many worries and anxieties about God would be avoided if we regarded him as a Father and if we abandoned ourselves to him. In a later chapter we will see how the structure of the movement of Theresian abandonment fits into the whole spiritual tradition, dispelling fear by making us live in a climate of joy and peace. Finally we will pause over the prayer of Thérèse which bathes in this movement of abandonment.

She sees herself as a weak little bird that wants to fly up to the sun, but that is beyond its *little strength: What will become of it? Will it die of sorrow, seeing itself so powerless. Oh no! the little bird is not going to torment itself. With bold abandon, it is going to stay staring up at the Divine Sun;* (Ms B 198). I do not think that there is a better definition of prayer than this last word.

7

The movement of abandonment

When we wander through Thérèse's writings, we can almost see her face on every page and we could apply each of her spiritual intuitions to a situation in our own lives. This is why it is difficult to make it fit into a system of spirituality: it is not easy to formulate a life. It is a little like crossing the Landes by train and passing near the pine forests. There is only one precise moment when you can take in clearly the whole panorama with a glance, before and after, you see only an indistinct mass.

It is the same with Theresian spirituality, there is only one point where the gaze can grasp clearly the coherence and connection of this doctrine and we think that this point is the movement of abandonment. Abandonment summarises her whole doctrine because it demands that we live as poor and needy, but certain that we are loved by an infinitely merciful Father. We can express it in another way: the heart of the Theresian message is faith in merciful Love and the road that leads us to this heart is the way of spiritual childhood which is lived in a particular way in the movement of abandonment.

It is truly abandonment which best opens the way to the loving kindness of God who has loved us first, since it is a question less of acting than of surrendering ourselves, less of giving than of receiving. We have seen that Christ's disciple accepts simply to be a poor child, to live in the arms of its Father in order to hand over to him every anxiety, every occupation and every limitation. Thérèse snug *in the arms of God* (Ms B 188), faces the storms without fear, for her Father is giving her *at each moment* what she needs.

Thérèse's disciple knows that while remaining little and weak, he or she can nourish great aspirations to sanctity. The great Gospel revelation is that God loves the little ones because they are little, poor and without courage. In a word, God loves empty hands. It is called the way of spiritual child-hood, but we must not be taken in, it is not a naive attitude that one adopts in order to be nice and free from care. Or perhaps we could call to mind the son who finds it quite natural to call on his father constantly with the undisturbed audacity of total confidence; this is the way to sanctity. And it is here that the movement of abandonment comes in, for this attitude must be lived, not in an intellectual way but in ordinary everyday life. We are going to try and put it back into the context of spiritual tradition.

Run or rest

All the spiritual writers who have spoken about abandon-ment have run the risk of being suspected of a certain quietism. We are thinking of Fénelon, of the Jesuit mystics who clarified Fr Lallemant (Rigoleuc and Surin), of Fr de Caussade and nearer our own day Dom Vital Lehodey. And yet they were in the very tradition of the Gospel. In the same way, when Thérèse died there were some prioresses of Carmels who rose up in arms against *Story of a Soul* because of this and under the pretext that it was a 'rose-water' doctrine. This is why we have to separate this understand-ing of abandonment from all its forgeries and from all its deviations.

We cannot do this better than by comparing Thérèse with another great spiritual leader who, while he cannot be accused of quietism, had even a reputation for being an out and out 'volontarist', St Ignatius of Loyola. We will see then that word for word, Thérèse uses the same expressions as he does. In the famous sentence of Ignatius which regulates the individual's part and God's part in action, we read: 'To entrust myself nobly to God, but to do all as if the success depended entirely on me and not on God. In other words, giving my whole attention to what I am doing, but as if I were doing nothing, and God alone was doing everything' (*Selected Sentences*). This axiom is not found anywhere in Ignatius' works, but it is a summary given by his disciples.

We find these two poles with Thérèse. We do firstly all that we can as if it depended on us and we expect everything as if it depended on God alone. We shall see further on what it means: 'To do all as if it depended on us', for the great obstacle here is that discouragement gives rise to a temptation against hope. But we will first quote Thérèse's word where she explains 'emphatically', says her sister Céline, 'that abandonment and confidence in God are nourished by sacrifice'.

> *We must*, she told me, *do all that is in our power, give without counting the cost, deny ourselves constantly, in a word, prove our love by all the good works that we can. But truly, how little it all is ... we must, when we have done all that we believe we have to do, consider ourselves 'unprofitable servants', hoping nevertheless that God will give us, by his grace, all that we desire. This is the hope of all little souls who 'run' in the way of spiritual childhood. I say 'run' and not 'rest'.*

I believe that we have here an admirable synthesis of the connection between God's action and our action, between grace and freedom. Nowhere does Thérèse stop asking us to go the whole way with love and she could say with Ignatius: 'love is proved first and foremost by deeds rather than words', but she also knew that we are poor and weak-willed and that one day we will make the discovery of our own powerlessness to love with all our heart. So she says *how little it all is* and we must expect everything from God, but on the condition that we have done all that we believe we have to do. Nowhere for Thérèse does 'leave it to God' correspond to 'take it easy'. We must run and not rest!

She made us confront our struggles

We must now look at the way Thérèse set about teaching her novices to help them live what I will call 'the harmony of opposites'. Let us note immediately that Thérèse is a realist; there is no denying a difficulty, evading the issue or trying to forget in feverish activity. An attitude that brings about repression would serve no purpose and only lead to disaster for 'one day the whole hardened block of tendencies will surface in the soul'.[1]

Thérèse did not want 'to step over the actual difficulty if it is necessary to pass under it'. *We are too little to put ourselves above our difficulties* (CSG). To pass under, is to sit in the difficulty and to live with it interiorly, that is to bear it because it contains the hidden meaning of our future. To pass over means always a sham exit.

Let us take a quick look at how Thérèse went about helping her sister Céline to live the movement of abandonment. Céline comes and complains to her sister Thérèse that her

---

1 We cannot do better here than invite the reader to reread pages 104ff of Victor Sion's book, *The Spiritual Realism of St Thérèse*, on the subject of deviations to avoid. He develops the subject at greater length than we do here.

companion in the novitiate has not filled the wood-box, when she herself carries out this duty with so much care. Our reaction would be to say: 'Pass over these pettinesses!' Thérèse takes another line by making her sister face up to the problem: 'Without trying to make me minimise the black picture I was painting before her eyes or trying to show it in a better light, she made me consider it closer and seemed to agree with me:

Well, then, let us say that your companion does have all the faults you say she has.

'Instead of trying to take our struggles away from us by refuting their causes, she made us face up to them' (CSG). Thérèse acted in this way because she wanted to help her sister to see reality and accept it. This is the first stage of the movement of abandonment. A person does not look for ways to side-step a duty, to run away from someone who has a difficult temperament and muse on something other than what we must live. He or she plunges into the everyday life such as it is because it is there that one becomes a saint. The divine life is nourished by the most ordinary everyday life. Abandonment is not a way of making life easier, but of helping us to make use of very little means when it is difficult.

She succeeded in making me love my lot

It is not enough to recognise the difficulty, because we can run away from it or take a dislike to it. We must moreover accept it and hold fast to it, in a word, love God's will which is communicated to us in these incidental occurrences. This is the evangelical meaning of 'the hour' or 'the chalice' that we are invited to drink. Thérèse sums up her teaching in a humorous image: *We have only to put up with the sudden showers patiently, it's too bad if we get a bit wet! We have to accept our weakness, for it is in it alone that God's power is displayed.*

This is the method Thérèse used with her sister Céline. Not only did she darken the picture, but she wanted to teach her how to love her situation: 'Little by little, she succeeded in making me love my lot, and even making me desire that the sisters be wanting in kindness to me ... Finally she would bring about in me the most perfect sentiments. Then, when this victory had been gained, she would hold up to me some unknown examples of virtue in the novice accused by me. Soon resentment gave way to admiration and I thought that the others were better than I was' (ibid.).

But very often in our life the difficulties and annoyances are more in our imagination than they are in reality. We build mountains out of imaginary worries. This is why, let it be said in passing, that we have to live in the present moment and not 'enlarge' problems with our imagination. This is how Thérèse went along with Céline, not without a good dose of humour. When she knew that the wood-box had been filled, unknown to her sister, she was careful not to let her know it so as not to take away her struggle:

'Sometimes, she used to let us have the surprise of an analogous discovery and she would profit from the occasion to show us that so often we bring these struggles on ourselves, because they do not exist in reality but are only pure imagination.'

If the struggle is real, we have to accept seeing it as it is and hand it over to God in confidence. When a difficulty arises in our life, we must not just stay with it, but bring about an immediate release so as to look at it with God. This is why we have to take it out of our heart very quickly so as to hand it over to God: *I read recently*, said Thérèse, *that the Israelites built the walls of Jerusalem working with one hand while holding a sword in the other. This is a good symbol of the interior dispositions we ought to have* (CSG).

If it is a question of a futile annoyance, we must not be afraid to look at it. It will then come to light and will fall of its own accord: 'I believe that in very important things, we do not overcome the obstacles. We stare at them, for as long as necessary, until, in cases where they come from the powers of illusion, they disappear' (Simone Weil).

'The bridge of loving confidence'

We are now at the third stage of the movement of abandonment. The further we advance the more we discover that we are empty-handed and far from God. We are separated from God by an abyss impassable for our own strength. Conrad de Meester has made a remarkable comparison to explain this situation: it is that of the 'bridge of hope'. It explains very well, as I said, the third stage of the rocket which will propel us into the arms of God:

'A bridge has to be thrown across this abyss. Two supports, one on each side, and based on solid foundations have to be erected. On our side there is humility whereby the finite creature humbly accepts its imperfections and its powerlessness. On the other side, that of the infinite God, the pylon is that of mercy in which we believe. Like humility, faith in God's merciful love is a necessary condition of hope. We cannot hope in someone and not believe in their goodness. The bridge of loving confidence is then thrown between the pylons enabling us to reach God. Or rather, God himself comes onto this bridge, takes hold of us and carries us to the other side' (*With Empty Hands* 93).

And this is where prayer comes in. Thérèse does not speak of it explicitly but on several occasions, we see her reaching in a movement of offering to God. Each time she experiences her weakness, she brings herself back to the feet of Jesus to offer him her momentary infidelities. She becomes aware of her limitations, she accepts them, she offers herself:

> *I hasten to say to God: My God, I know that I deserve this feeling of sadness; however let me offer it to you, just the same, as a trial that you have sent me through love. I am sorry for what I have done, but I am happy to have this suffering to offer you* (LC 3.7.2).

Basically, what is Thérèse saying? When things become too difficult and you feel incapable of rising above the mountains of pride and egotism which are in you, simply admit that you are *unprofitable servants*, hope for everything from God and he will give you everything through grace. This supposes that we call on God in prayer. This is the 'science of hope and confidence in God' that St Francis Xavier taught the young men setting out for the missions. It is necessary to read here a small forgotten book by St Alphonsus Ligouri: *The Great Means of Prayer*. His teaching is simple: when faced with the demands of the Gospel (to forgive our enemies, to be chaste, to be poor), we discover ourselves to be completely incapable, so there remains only one solution: to call on God confidently in humble persevering supplication.

All the spiritual masters affirm Christ's words: *What is impossible for men and women is possible for God* (Matt 19:26). We can have numerous excuses for our faults of weakness, but we never have any excuses for not praying: 'In fact, the grace of prayer is given to each one. It is always within our power to pray as soon as we wish' (St Alphonsus Ligouri). Men and women pray because they know that nothing is impossible for God: this is why they ask, search and knock (Mt 7:7). Here all the spiritualities agree for they have their origin in Christ's word in St John: *Without me you can do nothing* (Jn 15:5), but we know also that Jesus is with us until the end of time (Mt 28:28). And this is why we have recourse to him in intercession.

Such a prayer is born out of despair and hope, said the Curé of Ars: 'I often think that, when we come to adore Our Lord, we would obtain all that we wish, if we were to ask him with lively faith and a pure heart. But we are without faith, without hope, without desire and without love'. God always answers such a prayer in so far as it is made with faith and perseverance.

We will ask Thérèse how she used to pray at the beginning of this movement of abandonment and we will see that her prayer had two poles: the supplication of the child that expects everything from its Father, but who also rests in his arms because it knows that it is loved and heard. Thérèse loved especially that prayer of silence and abandonment where she was still beneath the gaze of the Father.

Her prayer is part of that great breathing movement of the Church's prayer. It is first of all a movement of supplication where we stretch out towards God through desire (*aspiration*). And then we rest in this gift by thanksgiving (*expiration*). So our supplication is the preparation for God's gift which reaches its fulfilment in praise:

It is gratitude which draws down most graces from God. He is moved and hastens to give us tenfold, and if we thank him with the same gratitude, what an incalculable multiplication of graces! I have experienced this, try it and you will see (CSG).

8

'What a great power is prayer'

We said that Thérèse's prayer springs from two sources: it is born in the midst of trial and suffering and is a cry of love or of supplication; or it is born in the midst of joy and is then a glance towards heaven, a cry of jubilation and gratitude. It is the very rhythm of Christian prayer: one breathes in and breathes out the breath of the Holy Spirit in the heart. We implore when we are in need and we give thanks when we are in joy.

We would like simply to include here two texts which emphasise this rhythm of Christian breathing. The first is from St Paul's letter to the Philippians. He invites the Christians to drive out all anxiety and to abandon themselves in supplication, for the Lord is near. Let us note in passing this movement of ascending and descending in the prayer.

The Lord is near. Do not be anxious about anything, but in everything, through prayer and supplication made with thanksgiving, make known your requests to God. And the peace of God which passes all understanding, will keep your hearts and minds in Jesus Christ (Phil 4:5-7).

We find something of the same rhythm in the preface of the Holy Spirit, regarding the prayer of the Church: 'Your Spirit upholds and keeps her faithful, so that she might never forget to call on you in the midst of trials, nor give thanks to you when she is in joy'.

The second text comes from Thérèse in manuscript 'C'. It is the first time that we have been struck by what she says about the power of prayer and we could draw from it here a whole lesson on prayer with Thérèse. As always, she speaks of prayer in relation to her personal experience, and here it is concerned with her liberty in prayer. She never allows herself to be confined by formulas but speaks freely to God as a child. She will insist very much on the power of supplication:

What a great power is prayer! It could be called a queen who has free access at every moment to the King and who can obtain whatever she asks ...

Then she gives a very personalised definition of prayer:

For me, prayer is an uplifting of the heart, a simple glance directed towards heaven, it is a cry of gratitude and of love in the midst of trial as well as joy, it is something great, supernatural, which expands my soul and unites me to Jesus (Ms C 242).

'All my strength comes from prayer and sacrifice'

In the struggles and temptations, Thérèse never relies on her own strength of will, but only on prayer and sacrifice. She knows only too well that it is impossible for her to grow up and that she must bear with herself such as she is, with all her imperfections (Ms A 207), but she also knows that God cannot inspire her with unrealisable desires, and she can therefore aspire to sanctity through the means of prayer.

We are faced with the same dilemma. We want to convert ourselves, to be gentle, good and pure and we become more and more discouraged for we see that we will never attain this. The risk is then to become saddened: *What is shameful, says Thérèse, is to spend one's time kicking one's heels instead of sleeping on the heart of Jesus.* Sr Geneviève comes to her downcast: 'I will never be good! *Yes, yes, you will get there,* she answered her, *God himself will see to it* (CSG). Like Sr Geneviève, we can be tempted to say: 'It's impossible. I am starting to get to know myself!' No, that is not the point. The important thing is not to know oneself, but to know God's efficacious love for us. This love is experienced, not in books, but through having recourse to him. Then what is difficult, what seems impossible, becomes attainable through recourse to God.

For this, we have to acquire a recourse reflex to God. We have to have recourse not once, but on every occasion, says St Paul. Everything depends on the strength of the request, that is the quality of the love which prompts the demand. This is when we bring into play those three dynamics of the Christian: faith, hope and charity. Little by little we must strengthen our triple relationship with God through recourse to him. At first it is weak and seldom, then it becomes more and more powerful, like everything that is lived and practised. We therefore need to make fervent requests and have recourse to God by desperate efforts and assaults of love. In this way prayer is born out of life itself and can become continual. But there are few people who have constant recourse to God.

Thérèse says that we must not be worried about the weakness of our first approaches. We must make this prayer: 'I believe, Lord, that at this moment you can give me strength for this battle because you love me.' Out of curiosity, I went back and reread the list of Thérèse's quotations for the word 'prayer' and I was struck by the insistence with which she notes the fervour and ardour of her prayer. And most of the time, she adds that her prayer was heard. We will include some of these quotations one after the other, they are impressive. They always correspond to situations where Thérèse could do nothing but have recourse to heaven:

> *I stayed there for a long time praying fervently* (Ms A 115). Concerning the Blessed Virgin, she says: *With what fervour did I not pray to her asking her to keep me always* (Ms A 123). To her prayer, she also joined concrete charity: *I was not satisfied with praying much for that sister ... I tried to render her all the services I could* (Ms A 222).

Thérèse recommends herself also to the prayers of others, this is very important when prayer becomes difficult or impossible. It does not matter whether the other prays or not, the intention is there: *I have written to Fr Pichon to ask for his prayers* (Ms A 76). *My prayers were very fervent* (Ms A 133). Thérèse knew also that her prayer would be heard if she prayed with faith, as Christ asks us to do in the Gospel (Mk 11:22-24). *I know that my prayer was heard* (Ms A 131). *We can help through prayer and sacrifice* (Ms A 252). *This is my prayer: I ask Jesus to draw me into the flame of his love* (Ms C 257).

Conscious of our weakness but boldly confident

We are going to live then in the most extraordinary relationship with God, one which is most authentic: asking him for the impossible, that is to say, the possibility of going along a road that humanly speaking is blocked. Where does this paradox come from? 'Go to God with empty hands, but everything will depend on the fervour of your request.' While remaining little, we are going to experience the power of Christ's word: *Everything that you will ask the Father in prayer; believe that you have already received it in faith* (Mk 11:24).

Such is the path of sanctity Thérèse of Lisieux maps out for us: *Sanctity does not consist in this or that practice, it consists in a disposition of heart which makes us humble and little in the arms of God, conscious of our weakness but boldly confident in his goodness as a Father.* We must develop a simple disposition to receive everything from God without ever possessing virtue or strength. Walking along such a road is not easy for it is necessary to have great confidence in God as a Father while being conscious of one's own weakness. And the temptation is to eliminate one part of the alternative to find tranquility.

It is both simple and not simple. The twofold difficulty is firstly to see ourselves very weak until the end of our life and then to have an audacious confidence in God. But this knowledge in itself is not enough. We have to make the effort, in a word: 'It is necessary to do it!' Do not complain about not succeeding. If you are happy to listen to Thérèse's words, without doing anything, then you no longer have the right to complain. As to attestations of success, I can provide you with thousands: those of St Thérèse of Lisieux and of all those who follow her way. I am thinking also of the Eastern monks.

Here again we find a fundamental and traditional attitude of Eastern spirituality: control of the thoughts by the frequent calling to mind of the Name of the Lord Jesus. At this precise point, all the spiritualities are in accord. There is in us a whole wave of desires, impressions and exterior events which put us into a whirlwind, and yet we have been baptised and the Risen Lord is living in us. So we train ourselves to remember Jesus (the living and active memory) within these thoughts. We allow them to surface in us, without repressing them, and we grasp hold of them in order to make them our own:

'The invocation makes it easy to keep watch over the heart: when a "thought", in the Gospel sense, rises up in the subconscious, we must, before it becomes an obsession, blot out with the Name the demoniacal suggestion and transfigure the energy thus liberated by clothing it with the same Name' (O. Clement *Questions sur l'homme*, 86).

'This movement is inspired by love' (St John of the Cross)

Since we are at the point where the movement of abandonment and the other spiritual currents converge, it is not useless to note that Thérèse belongs in the great line of Carmel. Those familiar with St John of the Cross will have recognised in the Theresian movement of abandonment the famous anagogical act which enables a person to rise above all created things. There is always the question of not stopping at secondary causes, without despising them, in order to cling to God's will. We go to God by detaching ourselves from all that is contingent. 'Such a movement,' says St John of the Cross, 'is inspired by love.' He defines it thus: 'When we feel the first movement of some vice, without delay we direct against this vice an act or movement of anagogical love which raises our affection to union with God' (*The Complete Works of St John of the Cross*, trans. A. Peers, Burns Oats, London 1957, vol. 3, p. 310).

Thérèse's advantage was that she understood this movement and lived it in her everyday life. She could then give a concrete interpretation of it to her novices, thereby helping them to avoid painful gropings. But her doctrine is in the same sanjuanist vein.

We could also draw a parallel with St Ignatius' examination of conscience. We do not mean the exercise that we sometimes call by this name and which consists in making, at the end of the day or in preparation for confession, an exact count of our faults, but it is the implementation of what we have said above. In this sense, it is necessary to link it firstly with spiritual discernment and the moral life. It means going to God with empty hands, in a spirit of thanksgiving, in order to recognise what he is doing in us. It could be defined as a throwing of one's whole being into the current of the Holy Spirit, so that his action may have greater sway, after inevitable failings. It is an active abandonment to the action of the Spirit within us. And this movement is on the plan of a perfect availability of a person to the action of God. It means a return to God, if only for a few moments, to bring before him our preoccupations, and our projects so that he will be the master in them.

When do we do it? From this viewpoint, we do it all the time. It is like an exercise of presence to God, but not outside of the action that we are doing or of our state in life. It is carried out in the action of the movement in order to purify our motives in doing it and to direct our intention towards God. It is more than presence to God, it is cooperation with God's action within us.

One day when Thérèse was speaking with Céline on the subject of union with God, the latter asked her a question: 'I asked her if she sometimes forgot the presence of God. She answered me quite simply: *Oh! no, I do not think I have ever been three minutes without thinking of God.* I manifested my surprise that such application was possible. She said: *We naturally think about someone we love!*' (CSG).

We are impressed by this extraordinary fact that 'Thérèse had never been three minutes without thinking of God'. And like Céline, we could be surprised that such application might be possible. And Thérèse replied to her that it is normal to think about someone we love. It is therefore in love lived on the level of existence, in the movement of abandonment, that it is necessary to look for the source of her union with God and her continual prayer.

It is certainly in this movement of abandonment that true union with God in action is to be found. And it is here that Thérèse certainly has a message for men and women of action who aspire to continual prayer, while they are immersed in an apostolic life. One seminary professor wrote to me recently: 'I am sometimes disturbed to see that the more "pious" are often not open apostolically and also that the more open risk becoming shallow and "mundane". Basically, many people, nay priests and religious, have a false idea about life and prayer. They think that life consists in bustling about and prayer consists in withdrawing somewhere to forget all about our neighbour and our human situation. This is a calumny of life and a calumny of prayer itself' (Mgr Anthony Bloom).

Thérèse again comes to tell us that it is not necessary to look for impossible conciliations, that continual prayer does not consist in having 'supporting thoughts', as if we had to ice our life with some bribes of prayer. What matters, Thérèse tells us, is that we know the depths of God's life with our whole human being (Eph 3:19). Thérèse never runs away from real life and it is with her whole being that she goes along to God lock, stock and barrel. As A. Bloom says: 'Prayer comes from two sources: either it is the wonderment of praise and thanksgiving, or it is the tragedy of supplication and intercession.'

In this precise sense her prayer is rooted in her movement of abandonment, one could say of her what was said of Ignatius of Loyola that he was 'a contemplative in action'. It is at the very heart of her life and of her work with the novices that she prays unceasingly. Union with God is not to be found in a psychological division. If the heart is detached from itself and entirely abandoned to God, it prays unceasingly. Thérèse, in her weakness, feels the strength of God; on condition that she expresses this weakness and acknowledges it, she experiences the presence and the power of the Lord Jesus. This is the origin of the tradition of the

Jesus Prayer of the East which makes the Lord present in the whole of our human being: 'That my humanity', said Teilhard, 'might become a field of experience for the Holy Spirit.' We could also speak of the vigilance of the heart. St Benedict says that the monk must avoid forgetfulness of God and crush all his thoughts on the rock of Christ.

To conclude, we would like to call to mind another 'theological place' of spirituality: 'the present moment' (Fr de Caussade), but we shall return to it. It is, with the movement of abandonment and the anagogical act, the special place where we meet God for it is there that he reveals his will in the fabric of our life. Thérèse will explain it clearly concerning her profession retreat:

> *I have noticed many times that Jesus does not want to give me provisions, he nourishes me at every moment with food that is always new, I find it within me without knowing how it got there ... I believe quite simply that it is Jesus himself hidden in the depths of my poor little heart who is giving me the favour of acting in me and making me think of what he wishes me to do at the present moment* (Ms A 165).

I have always loved this word of St Alphonsus Rodriguez, the porter of Majorca, which sums up so well Thérèse's act of abandonment: 'When I feel some bitterness within me, I put this bitterness between God and me and I pray until he changes it into sweetness'. It means always looking this bitterness in the face, putting it between our hands and offering it to the Lord who transforms the obstacle into means. In the spiritual life, we can be deprived of prayer time, of the Eucharist and of other spiritual means, but we can never make excuses for not interiorly placing ourselves in God's hands in the purification of the heart. Thérèse tells us that this is a source of profound freedom where we find true joy.

111

9

The prayer of abandonment

We said earlier that Thérèse's prayer had as it were two poles: an ascending movement of supplication which corresponded with aspiration and a descending movement more centred on praise and abandonment. A text that illustrates and summarises this movement very well comes in the writings at the time when Thérèse is speaking about prayer:

The Blessed Virgin shows me that she is not displeased with me, she never fails to protect me as soon as I invoke her. If I have a concern, an embarrassment, very quickly I turn towards her and she always takes care of my needs, as the tenderest of mothers. How many times when speaking to the novices have I invoked her and felt the benefits of her maternal protection! (Ms C 243).

But it is at the second pole that we would like to stop today, the most important in Thérèse's life, where she defines prayer as a glance directed towards heaven, *a cry of gratitude and of love in the midst of trial as well as joy ... which expands my soul and unites me to Jesus* (Ms C 242).

Thérèse's prayer is strongly marked by the movement of abandonment which she practises and lives day after day. It can be said that it is mystical prayer in the real sense of the word, that is to say prayer where God's action takes precedence over our activity. Let us never forget that prayer

113

is the exact reflection of the spiritual life. And St John of the Cross has well noted that the passage between a spiritual life predominantly active and a life predominantly passive is marked by a simplification of prayer and an impossibility to meditate or reflect.

It is not extraordinary graces which make a life mystical, as Fr Molinié says with humour, 'these graces belong in the stage property-room'. It must be recognised that in Thérèse's life, there were very real mystical graces, but they were purely interior: on one occasion, she experienced the fire of divine love burning her own heart. But the essence of her mystical life was that active and living passivity which took place in an atmosphere of peace. She felt that she was carried along by God's love as a child is carried in its father's arms. She was sure that nothing could happen to her because she *knew in whom she had put her trust* (2 Tim 1:12).

What appears above all in Thérèse's writings when she speaks of prayer is the prayer of quiet, of silence and of peace. She is there beneath the Father's gaze, with a very keen awareness of being loved by him, living with that tenderness that fills her and also goes beyond her. From the moment Thérèse's heart is taken beyond her own concerns, saying like Abraham, *God will provide*, one could say that she became a mystic, without her being obviously aware of it.

A prayer in naked faith

It must not be thought that Thérèse was swimming in consolations and that she was always very keenly aware of this presence of God. Like each of us, she knew obscure states of dryness and she experienced the absence of God. When she went on her profession retreat, she admitted that she knew what awaited her and said with humour: *Jesus is going to sleep as usual*. But the fact that she complains of God's

114

absence is the sign that God is at work in her! To feel his absence, it is necessary to know his presence. To experience God as distant, it is necessary that he be present in the heart in a hidden way.

But we must emphasise above all the way Thérèse reacts in her periods of darkness. She could have become strained, wishing at all costs to bring about this presence of God through forced sentiments of the will or the imagination, but she never reacts in this manner. In her prayer, as in her everyday life, she brings into play abandonment or rather the dynamism of abandonment. I invite you to have the same experience.

You are believers, assured that God loves you tenderly. You come to prayer and you are like a dumb beast before God. Instead of forcing God's hand to make him come to you, you say to him simply: 'Father, I abandon myself to you, do with me what you will. Whatever you do to me, I thank you. I am ready for all, I accept all.' You have no doubt recognised Charles de Foucauld's very beautiful prayer of abandonment? Say it to the end and you will experience a great relaxation take place in you, a feeling of peace and sweetness will come upon you, far exceeding all sensible consolation.

I know people who were once locked in their difficulties yet experienced within them a feeling of release the moment they realised that they were not masters of their life and that God was holding them in his hands. This does not take away any of their personal responsibility, but it puts it in second place in relation to God's action.

You are going to live Thérèse's paradox: dry prayer can become very nourishing and can make you experience the true joy of God. A word of St John of the Cross has always impressed me: 'The soul does not go to prayer to tire itself, but to relax.' And he was not one who encouraged seeking sensible consolations at prayer! Speaking of Thérèse, her sister Céline said: 'Her whole life was spent in naked faith. There was not a soul less consoled in prayer; she confided to me that she had spent seven years in the most arid prayer: her annual retreats, her monthly retreats were a trial for her. And yet one would have thought her inundated with spiritual consolations, judging from the unction of her words and deeds, and her union with God.'

For a Carmelite who has to spend four or five hours each day in prayer, we gauge what must have been the trial Thérèse had to undergo of seven years of arid prayer. But it is here that we come to grips with the dynamism of abandonment: 'Despite that state of dryness, continued her sister, she was only more assiduous at prayer, *even happy that through it she could give more to God*. She would not allow us to steal a single moment from this holy exercise and this was how she formed her novices.' In prayer, Thérèse therefore seeks God for himself alone. From this point of view, the dryness is useful because it assures her that she is not going to prayer for the ideas or sentiments she might find there, but for God alone, whatever the sentiments accompanying the prayer. In this way the driest prayer developed in Thérèse 'affectus fidei', a love of faith of which the spiritual writers speak. Céline said it was thought that she was inundated with spiritual consolations, judging from the unction of her words and her deeds, and her union with God.

She goes to God simply to be with him and to give herself *'more'* – this is her expression – to love. Thus in her relations with God, as in her relations with her sisters, she comes to distinguish true sentiment from sheer emotivity in which we too often enclose prayer and fraternal life. This is a true discernment which verifies Thérèse's life of prayer and her love for her sisters. It comes from an ever greater attachment to God and to others, loved and wanted for themselves. When

116

a person accepts to cross this desert, God can fill him or her with sweetness and they experience real consolation, that of the Holy Spirit: 'Consoler best, most delightful guest of our souls, refreshing coolness ... Come, fill the inmost depths of the hearts of your faithful.'

'I say simply to God what I want to say' (Ms C 242)

We understand then that Thérèse experiences liberty in prayer. She is no longer attached to one form of prayer, she has no need to go searching in books for beautiful formulas written for the occasion. And she adds with humour: *I have not the courage to force myself to search in books for beautiful prayers, there are so many of them it would give me a headache!* (Ms C 242). How close she is to us, this saint whose head would ache from so many prayers and, dare we say it, from so much twaddle!

When we are in someone's arms, we do not say: 'Wait a moment while I go and find in a manual what I must say to you!' It is simply enough to let one's heart speak. Once the basic harmony is established between us, one can strike all the other chords of his or her instrument, says Fr Surin. But it takes a long time for the Holy Spirit to bring us into the embrace of the Father and the Son. Lovers remain long hours in each other's arms, without speaking. A single word could interrupt this intimacy and break the fine thread of tender relationship.

St Bernard will say *in Sermon VIII* in his *Commentary* (on The Song of Songs) 'that this mutual knowledge of the Father and the Son, this reciprocal love is nothing other than the sweetest kiss, but also the most secret'. The person who receives the Spirit receives this kiss and enters into the embrace of the Trinity. And, he adds: 'John drew from the

117

heart of the only Son what the latter had drawn from his Father's heart. We can also hear within us the Spirit of the Son, calling 'Abba! Father'. If carnal marriage joins two beings together in one flesh, all the more so does spiritual union join them in one spirit.'

This is the very essence of prayer for it is the time of the engagement when one gives one's full attention to the other and when each one finds great joy in the other. It is not without feeling that we are guilty of a certain indiscretion that we stealthily enter into Thérèse's prayer and one is always afraid of using the coarse language of our human experiences to speak about inexpressible things. And yet Thérèse throws out hints to us through certain confidences that she was allowed to experience the Father's word to Jesus: *You are my beloved Son. In you I am well-pleased.*

One day when her sister Céline entered her cell — we will return to this later — she found her sister praying the 'Our Father', with great recollection. And with tears in her eyes. Céline adds: 'She loved God as a child dearly loves its Father with outbursts of incredible tenderness. During her illness it happened when she was speaking about God, she used the word *Papa*. We began to laugh, but she said with deep emotion: *Oh! yes, he is indeed my 'Papa' and how sweet it is for me to call him by this name.*

We think here naturally of what Paul says in his letter to the Romans: *You have received a Spirit that makes you adoptive sons and daughters and through which we cry out: 'Abba! Father!* (8:5). It is the familiar child's word 'Papa', unknown in the religious vocabulary of Judaism, and it is the expression of the filial intimacy, full of familiarity and tenderness of Jesus for his Father.'

Thérèse, in her prayers, continues Jesus' dialogue with his Father, concerning all humanity. And the essence of her prayer is constituted by a single word, 'Father', which is in her consciousness as it was in Jesus, on all-occasions: *Father, I thank you that you have heard me ... Father, I bless you for having hidden these things from the wise and the prudent ... Father, I praise you ...*

But in this very simple dialogue, there is a place for the whole gamut of sentiments and exchanges, as one does with a friend who is listening to us and loves us. We speak familiarly and say everything that is in our heart and touches our own life: *I do what children who do not know how to read do,* says Thérèse, *I say quite simply to God what I want to say to him, without beautiful phrases and he always understands me* (Ms C 242).

'I recite an 'Our Father' very slowly' (Ms A 243)

With Thérèse, there is a mutual play between prayer of the heart and prayer of the lips. One could think, after all that we have said, that Thérèse did not like vocal prayer. We need to understand the meaning of her words. Like Christ in the Gospel, she could not stand a wearisome reiteration of words, as if it were necessary to speak much to make oneself better understood. The Father knows what we need, there is no need to remind him with a flood of words. This is why Thérèse's prayer is constituted essentially by loving silence. She silences all her personal circuits in order to give her attention to listening to God. And it is when she is silent that God can speak to her. Thérèse is real and she is not drawn to 'sublime' ready-made prayers. But she has said herself that she loved the Divine Office.

Moreover, she experienced what our Eastern brothers and sisters say of the Jesus prayer. They advise a person who is beginning to pray to recite slowly the formula. 'Lord Jesus,

Son of God, Saviour, have mercy on me, a sinner', in such a way that the prayer of the lips gradually kindles the prayer of the heart. The sign that this prayer has gone from the head to the heart is that the person experiences within them a certain sweetness, or better still a fire, that of the Holy Spirit. Thérèse did not know the Jesus prayer, but she is returning here a great traditional law of prayer.

A man such as Julien Green speaks of that state produced by the recitation of certain prayers. He describes it thus in his *Journal*: 'One does not learn to pray from a book, any more than one learns to speak English or German through books. One can note here however something that many authors overlook and it is that there is a moment when the person who prays suddenly loses his or her footing. Even recited prayers sometimes lead there. What does it mean to lose one's footing? It means that one no longer knows what one is doing and that it no longer matters. It is a little like the second when one falls asleep. How many times I have been on the look-out for that moment of falling asleep! But it comes without our knowing it, and I think that the same can be said for prayer with or without words' (J. Green, *Vers l'invisible*, p. 111).

Thérèse experienced this usual occurrence in the life of prayer, according to the principle stated above, to know that one is thinking about the Other before troubling about oneself. And she experienced that above all in periods of dryness:

Sometimes when my mind is in such dryness that it is impossible for me to draw forth one thought to unite myself to God, I recite very slowly an 'Our Father' and then the angelic Salutation. These prayers carry me away, they nourish my soul so much more than if I had recited them quickly one hundred times (Ms A 243).

120

What is happening when a person says slowly the words of the 'Our Father'? By means of striking the heart with the very words of Christ, they transpierce it and bring forth the Spirit hidden in the depths of the heart, of which they were not even aware. This is something like what Paul says in Romans (8:26): *When we do not know what words to choose in order to pray* (when we do not have words), *the Spirit prays in us with groanings too deep for words.*

To those who labour strenuously at prayer, I would like to give this simple advice of Thérèse. Take a full hour and the text of the 'Our Father' — for time is needed to become recollected and attentive, capable of persevering or holding out in prayer with one single word. When silence has been achieved so that the Spirit might come in, repeat Jesus' prayer to his Father, saying slowly: 'Our Father who art in heaven! Stay contemplating this word for as long as you will find meaning, comparisons, relish and consolation in considerations relating to this word' (St Ignatius, *Exercises* no 252). Then go on and do the same with the other words of the 'Our Father'. There is no doubt that you will not come to the end of the text before the hour is up, it does not matter! The essential thing is not to meditate on Christ's words, but to impress them in your heart and to pray them with your lips. And when you say: 'Hallowed be thy Name', turn around this word and say it in another way: 'Sanctify your Name', 'Show yourself Holy'! During this prayer, it is necessary to gaze at Christ and hold onto the words, rejecting every other image or thought. You will overcome boredom. But know that once you come out from the prayer, you will surprise your heart 'by catching it red-handed at prayer'. This way of praying is very nourishing for a life of union with God.

Thérèse understands this from experience and when she begins to say the 'Our Father', she stops and is not able to go any further. She already understands what we will see in eternity. In a word, she already has a foretaste of heaven on earth and she does not know what more she will have in heaven than she already possesses on earth. She fully attained the goal Teresa of Avila set her daughters when she invited them to pray. One day when someone was speaking in front of Thérèse of Lisieux about magnetisers and hypnotisers, she exclaimed: *How I want to be magnetised by Jesus!* Essentially, praying, for the great Teresa as for the little one, is accepting to put oneself for one hour beneath the fulgurating rays of God's gaze, which penetrate to the depths of the heart, like a laser.

I am surprised today when I see so many religious men and women running after all the Eastern techniques – which I do not despise – in order to learn how to pray. I want to say to them: 'Do not go and look at the Hindu side too much, look rather at your dog who is waiting for its master's return, and you will know what it is to wait for the return of Jesus Christ and therefore to pray!' It is not strange to be a poor dog who can do nothing to get itself out of the situation of waiting, for it does not have anything to distract it while it is waiting its master's coming. It is obliged to be bored until it sees him coming.

I am thinking here of Teresa of Avila. She was 67 years old, on the eve of her death, lying on her straw mattress. Fr Anthony of Jesus was bringing her the Blessed Sacrament. She had the strength to sit up and looking at the Eucharistic Christ said: 'At last, my Beloved, we are going to see each other, it is time for us to be on the way.' But Thérèse was on the way as soon as she began to pray.

Such is the prayer of abandonment with Thérèse: 'One day, I went into the cell of our dear Sister and I was struck by her expression of great recollection. She was sewing away and yet seemed lost in deep contemplation:

122

'What are you thinking about?' I asked her.

I am meditating on the Our Father, she replied. *It is so sweet to call God our Father! ...* And there were tears in her eyes' (CSG).

To conclude, I would like to cite a text full of humour given by Henri Bremond. It could be applied to Thérèse and to all those little ones to whom the mysteries of the kingdom are revealed. It illustrates very well what we have tried to say so imperfectly here:

'The Mother of Ponçonnas, the foundress of the reformed Bernadines in Dauphin, was at Ponçonnas, during her childhood, and she came across a poor cowherd who seemed to her to be so rustic that she thought she had no knowledge of God. She drew her aside and wholeheartedly set about instructing her. This wonderful girl begged her with many tears to teach her what she had to do to finish her 'Our Father', for, said she in her mountain dialect: 'I do not know how to come to the end. From the time I was nearly five years old, whenever I say the word 'Father', and think that he who is above, said she raising her finger, that same one is my Father, I weep and remain the whole day in that state minding my cows' (*Histoire du Sentiment religieux*).

10

Thérèse discovers a new way

The life of a saint is constantly evolving and Thérèse's life was no exception to this law of growth. She never sought to know where she was in her journey, for she did not wish to store up merits. It did not matter to her whether she died young or old, her *one desire is to please Jesus* (Ms C 208). But in the evening of her life, when she is singing the mercies of the Lord in her regard, by writing the Story of her soul, she looks back on the different stages she has passed through. When writing, she puts herself before God by examining the movements of his work in her so as to retain the memory mentally and to know the direction he is inspiring her to follow.

It is from the summits that she contemplates the sequence of the important stages of her life. She understands with joy that all the moments of her human destiny have been trans-figured by God's action in her and she gives thanks for it. It is not our intention here to describe the curve of her journey, which is different for each saint. Others have done this very well for Thérèse, and we think here of Conrad de Meester in his book *With Empty Hands*. We wish simply to take one stage which seems fundamental for our interest here, to know the moment when she entered into what she calls her *little way that is totally new* (Ms C 207). This is, when she began her movement of abandonment.

The discovery of the movement of abandonment is linked with her becoming aware of her new way, a way that is very straight and very short (Ms C 207). What allows us to affirm the connection between a 'new way' and 'abandonment', is that the same expression is to be found in the two texts where she speaks of abandonment and of her little way. She refers to *the arms of God or of Jesus*. Let us quote these two texts to refresh our memory.

The first where she speaks of abandonment:

Jesus was pleased to show me the only way which leads to that divine furnace, this way is the abandonment of the little child that sleeps without fear in its Father's arms (Ms B 188).

And the second text is enriched by two new images, that of the lift and the stairway which will be Jesus' arms:

I wanted to find a lift that would take me up to Jesus, for I am too little to climb the rough stairway of perfection ... the lift that must take me up to heaven are your arms, O Jesus (Ms C 207,208).

To rely on nothing

But we will come back to that stage of abandonment in Thérèse's spiritual journey. Let us forget a little the way, but profit just the same from her teaching. We need to understand what she means so that we might remain flexible when God invites us to submit in order to enter upon this way of abandonment.

Thérèse has always wanted to be a great saint and she came to Carmel for Jesus alone. She adds that the Lord gave her the grace not to have any illusion and to find in Carmel life just as it was: that demands great realism for a 15-year-old! From the dawn of reason, Thérèse gave herself to God without reserve, but she could not avoid wanting this perfection in a way that was a little too human and too active. We all dream of a sanctity won by sheer strength of arm. She learns through experience that she cannot rely on anything; neither her merits, nor her will, nor her human resources.

But it is normal to make plans for sanctity, to mortify oneself so as to attain our set goal: God himself and his sanctity. We are always tempted to want to lay hold of God by means of our works, our asceticism and our prayer: all these attitudes are false moves. We must not lift up our hands to seize God, rather we must lower them in a movement of welcome and desire. We have to desire God with all the strength of our being, while renouncing any desire to conquer him.

Thérèse brought into play all her human resources, but she very quickly realised that it was all so little. In our need for activity undertaken for sanctity there is much self-love, above all there is an instinct to possess and to achieve which contains a fair amount of pride. *Ah! there you go again wanting riches, to possessions! To lean on these is like leaning on a piece of red-hot iron* (CSG).

And this is why in our relations with God as in our relations with others, our best desires have to be purified. I will say: the more elevated the goal envisaged, the more our intentions have to be scoured, like the climbing-shoot of the vine. Then God sets to work in us − he has never ceased acting really − to try and make us understand that we have miscalculated the expense involved. We have to understand that God is not only the goal towards which we are directing all our efforts but that he is also the source from which they spring.

For many of us, an important work of grace is required to make us understand this: and this is the work of the passive purifications described by St John of the Cross. Crises more or less severe come into our life – whether it be from our psychological tensions or external events, it does not matter! – the important thing is that we discover through experience that God is all and we are nothing. In fact, God ploughs in us the soil of humility so that he can make the grain of sanctity germinate. There would be one way to escape these crises, and that would be to descend lower than the earth so that God would have nothing to level. In a word, the humble have nothing to fear in this domain.

Thérèse was profoundly humble. Let us recall her last words, on her death-bed: *Yes, it seems to me that I am humble, I have only sought the truth.* She understood very quickly that God did everything, that she could do nothing, except give him her consent. 'Because St Thérèse of the Child Jesus was so humble, she felt herself incapable of climbing the rough stairway of perfection and so she set about becoming ever more little, so that God might take care of her affairs and carry her in his arms, as happens in families, to all little children. She wanted to be a saint, but without growing up.'

Although she was very humble, Thérèse was not spared from experiencing her own powerlessness. Her best desires had to pass through the crucible of purification. She understood clearly what an old Trappist chaplain said to the monks: 'God does all, but he depends on us that he might do all.' When she spoke of the rough stairway of perfection, she was not able to forget that when she was a child, she could not climb the staircase alone, without calling out at each step: *'Mamam! Mamam!'* (Letter of Mme Martin to Pauline, Nov. 1875).

'I can therefore, despite my littleness, aspire to sanctity' (Ms C 207)

This is how she expresses herself on this subject to Mother Marie de Gonzague. The text is fundamental in Thérèse's journey, we have cited some extracts, it has to be read in its entirety:

> You know, Mother, I have always desired to be a saint, but alas! I have always noticed, when I compare myself with the saints, that there is between them and me the same difference that exists between a mountain whose summit is lost in the heavens and the obscure little grain of sand trampled underfoot by the passers-by; it is impossible for me to grow up, I have to bear with myself just as I am, with all my imperfections, but I want to search for a way to go to heaven by a little way that is very straight, very short, a totally new way (Ms C 207). And it is the discovery of the lift!

Once she becomes aware of her own powerlessness, her imperfections and, above all, when she accepts herself as she is, God can show himself to Thérèse as the One who is ready to do all the work. In the beginning, she is seeking to walk towards God and especially to love him; in the end, she understands that it is enough to let herself be loved by him. This implies that she had a very profound light on the quite foolish dimension of God's love for her. Thérèse did not decide one fine day to enter upon the *little way* and to abandon herself to God; but on 9 June 1895, she received *the grace to understand more than ever before how much Jesus desired to be loved* (Ms A 180).

Hence the extraordinary discovery that she made. She understood that God was love and that he was kneeling at his creatures' feet to ask: 'Do you want this love?' It was no longer a question for Thérèse to love God but to let herself be loved by him. And we can understand how she wrote the page following that word on abandonment: *Oh! how sweet is the way of Love! ... how I wish to apply myself to do always God's will with the greatest abandonment* (Ms A 181).

To discover this love, is again a conversion. We do not turn towards God, but God is always turning himself towards us in Jesus Christ and asking us to welcome this love by surrendering ourselves to him. When a person has realised that God has loved him first and that this love has been acting in his own life, only one thing remains for him to do: to let himself be loved by God. As soon as Thérèse glimpsed this face of love, a certain number of words and expressions became important for her: abandonment, silence, listening, looking at, being attentive, offering no resistance ... All that must have a value in God's sight because it is only by means of these that we are permitted to receive God and to reflect infinity. St Irenaeus said: 'The attribute of God is to do, and for us to offer no resistance' *(Against the Heresies)*.

Thérèse explains this very well in a letter to her sister Céline: *When Jesus has looked on a soul, immediately he gives it his divine likeness, but the soul must not cease fixing its gaze on him* (LT 134). Thérèse received during the course of her life some mystical graces of this kind. Let us think of the one of 9 June 1895 when she discovered merciful Love, without forgetting that of 14 June 1895. She was in the Choir beginning the Way of the Cross:

When I suddenly felt myself wounded by a fire so ardent that I thought I would die. I do not know how to explain it, it was as if an invisible hand had plunged me entirely into the fire. Oh! what fire and what sweetness at the same time! I was on fire with love, and I thought that one moment, one second more, I would not have been able to bear it without dying.[1]

There is another grace which is seldom spoken of because she situates it at the beginning of her religious life, at the time of the reception of the habit, in July 1889. However, it is interesting to note, for Thérèse says at the end a word

---

1 Thérèse gave an account of this grace to her sister Mother Agnes on 7 July 1897, cf. *Her Last Conversations*, 7.7.2 (translator).

which explains the follies of love which some saints can accomplish. It is a grace which belongs to the 'flight of the spirit' which pulls the person away from his or her normal life. It is when she went to pray in the garden in the hermitage of St Magdalene, she is plunged into deep recollection:

> *It was as if a veil had been thrown over all the things of earth ... I felt myself entirely hidden beneath the veil of the Blessed Virgin. At that time, I had charge of the refectory and I remember doing things as if I was not doing them: it was as if I was acting with a borrowed body. I remained in that state for the whole week. God alone can put us into it and it can sometimes detach a soul from earth for ever* (LC 11.7.2).

'Oh! it's not that!'

One understands after such graces that it is enough to detach a person from earth. It is told that St Ignatius of Loyola was being tormented by temptations against chastity. One day the Blessed Virgin showed herself to him and he admitted that afterwards he had never more been tempted in this domain. When we read the life of Thérèse of Lisieux, we are in admiration at seeing the quality of her love, her spirit of renunciation in all that she did. One day when she was suffering morally (because of the trial of faith, at the end of her life) and also physically, someone spoke about heroism in front of her. And she replied: *Oh! no, it is not that!*

In this answer, there is not only a correction, there is also the suffering of someone who is not understood, as Christ suffered from the hardness of his apostles' hearts because they did not understand anything. It is as if she said: 'You do not understand anything about it ... You have missed the point.' You think that it is the heroism that comes from a 'will of iron', as a preacher said one day about Thérèse. No, it is not that! If I dare, I would say that she was not

131

able to do otherwise. There is something other in Thérèse, which is no longer of the earth and which is dependent on the Spirit of Pentecost. From the day when Love penetrated her whole being, she has been surrounded and transformed by him.

As Fr Molinié, OP, says: 'Heaven fell on her head' and from that day, Thérèse, like all the other saints, was capable of the greatest follies for God, to deliver her body to the flames or like Fr Kolbe to offer his life in exchange for another prisoner. In other words, it is the power of God, the 'dynamis tou theou' of which St Paul speaks which clothes her. What other explanation is there for the attitude of Thérèse and that of Fr Kolbe. With heroism, he could have offered his life, but not transform that starvation bunker into a place where all those living dead sang hymns. These men and women have to be suddenly brought face to face with heaven, with the Spirit of Pentecost in order to do such things.

We say sometimes: 'I could never do what Fr Kolbe did!' And we are all the same if strength from above and the power of God has not been given to us. But the day when the face of the risen Christ is shown to us, we will be capable of everything. St Perpetua suffered terribly in prison, from the pains of childbirth; and the goaler said to her: 'What will it be tomorrow in the arena?' She replied then: 'Today it is I who am suffering, tomorrow another will suffer in me!'

Then let us not say: 'If I had but one tenth of Thérèse's will, I would achieve it!' That is not the question and in this domain, Thérèse knew only too well that she was as poor as we are. Our admiration for the courage of the saints would make them smile for they have been moved and impelled by the power of the risen Jesus who gave them his spirit.

To abandon oneself into the arms of the Father

When one has received such a revelation of God's love, one is capable of everything and the first step is to abandon oneself to his action. It is as if God were saying to us: 'I love you much more than you suspect, let me take the helm, hand over all the control buttons to me. This is what happens when a ship passes through the Suez canal: the captain has to leave the helm in the hands of the pilot. This is one of the best images of faith and confidence that I know!

Thérèse uses the comparison of the lift. *We live in an age of inventions, now we no longer have to take the trouble to climb up a staircase; in the homes of the wealthy a lift replaces it advantageously* (Ms C 207,208). We will see in the next chapter that two or three years before, Thérèse had said to Sr Marie of the Trinity who was discouraged precisely when confronted with the stairway of perfection she had to climb: *Soon conquered by your futile efforts God will come down himself and, taking you in his arms, will carry you forever in his Kingdom* (Testimony of Sr Marie of the Trinity at the Apostolic Process, Bayeux).

What does it mean to abandon oneself to God? It is something other than going up towards him, it is much more profound. It meant the total dissolution of Thérèse's will in the will of God. It is what Fr de Caussade, with all the spiritual writers, calls abandonment to divine Providence.

To help us understand the difference between the total gift and abandonment, Thérèse tells the story of Blessed Suso. He was a lover of wisdom and used to mortify himself in a terrible way in order to obtain this wisdom. One day an angel appeared to him and said: 'Until now you have been a simple soldier, now I am going to make you a knight. Give up all these mortifications and no longer decide anything

133

for yourself. I will order everything.' On reading this story, Thérèse of the Child Jesus said: *I was a knight straightway*. She was so humble and therefore purified enough – as we have seen above – not to have known these struggles where we want to rival God in generosity. She had never decided anything for herself and each time God touched her, she offered no resistance. This is why she obtained all that she asked for. God resists our requests because we dispute with him. Henri Suso received a light – perhaps because of his preceding struggle – to understand something subtle and very demanding, but of another order. Thérèse had been brought face to face with this light early in the piece, while blessed Suso had only been given it later.

In conclusion: if we wish to enter upon the way of abandonment – some even make a vow to do so – we must desire this light and earnestly ask for it. God cannot refuse us, if we express it this way: 'If it pleases you, Lord, show me the Face of your Mercy. And now, I thank you for having granted it!' Then we will be able, like St Paul, to fight the real fight, the good fight, not the struggle of which we so often dream. May we, like Thérèse, be knights straightway, even if today we are still in the second class.

The act of abandonment

The act by which we cease to walk towards God in order to abandon ourselves to him is purely interior. It is a completely free decision to give preference to God's ways and action in us. Thus abandonment is dependent on the *obedience of faith* of which Paul speaks on two occasions in the letter to the Romans (1:5) and (16:26). We become one in our innermost being with the attitude of Christ and with all the witnesses of the faith who say: *Here I am, O God, I come to do your will!*

But because we are flesh and spirit, this interior decision must take form in an act which means in God's eyes and in our own, that we have decided to live henceforth a life of abandonment. It does not matter what formula is used, but it would be put in words which correspond to the interior decision. For we, living in time and space, need to renew this act, because our liberty fluctuates. Some will renew this gift each day at Communion and others at the important stages of their life (retreats, recollection days, etc.).

The formula varies according to the interior decision. It would be best for each to compose their own act of abandonment as Thérèse did with the Act of Love. The prayer of Charles de Foucauld, Thérèse's Act of Offering to Merciful Love or a consecration to the Blessed Virgin could be used. Some, more familiar with the Exercises of St Ignatius, will take the 'Suscipe'. It is always preferable to make it at the end of a retreat and prepare for it by means of different meditations or contemplations directing us towards abandonment.

The essential thing in this is that we give ourselves to God 'carte blanche' so that his will might be fulfilled in us and that we give our whole-hearted consent to it. We can be helped to live this attitude of faith by reading chapters 11 and 12 of the letter to the Hebrews: *By faith, answering the call, Abraham obeyed and set out for a country that he was to receive as his inheritance, and he set out not knowing where he was going* (Heb 11:8).

Properly speaking, this Act when it is made on an initiative of God, marks an entry into a mystical life. The essence of this life does not consist in extraordinary phenomena, but in a predominance of the Spirit's action in us. We must no longer decide anything for ourselves and wait for God to prompt us through the action of his grace. We become very much aware that our whole life is directed and moved by the Holy Spirit.

From this comes the prayer of quiet and of silence. Like Agar, we say in our prayer: *You are a God who sees* (Gen 16:13). And as soon as an anxiety arises in our life or in our prayer, we say like Abraham: *God provides* (Gen 22:14). It is difficult to describe such prayer when one does not live it oneself. Fr Lallemant says on this subject that there is the same difference between the lived and the spoken word as there is between a lion seen in a painting and a lion seen in real life.

I will not say that such prayer is without difficulty for we can often have the impression that we are wasting our time, but I dare to say that it is easy in the sense that it is freely given to us and we can find it within us without effort. It is said of St Ignatius that, towards the end of his life, 'he was able to find God whenever he wished, no matter at what hour' (*Autobiography* no. 99). He had only to set himself to pray in order to be conscious again of God's presence, like Thérèse who was never three minutes without thinking about God, because she loved him. I desire and pray that this grace, prepared for all those who make the act of abandonment, might be given them in all its fullness, according to their state.

11

The temptation against hope and abandonment

Now we would like to reply to a practical question that all who are following Christ ask themselves. One day or other, we come to the end of our resources in our journey towards God and we feel our strength deserting us: *You will never reach perfection, she used to say to me often: you want to climb a mountain and God wants to make you go down to the bottom of the fertile valley where you will learn to despise yourself* (CSG). So many of the ups and downs of life make us ask the question which comes from a tension between these two attitudes, 'to climb up' or 'to go down'. It is then the fundamental problem of hope which is going to confront us.

To climb up or to go down

Thérèse gives us the solution in her Manuscripts. What I am about to say will be a commentary on her message gained through her struggles. To profit from this message, you have to be tempted in the domain of hope and confidence. I will say that this is almost the only temptation in life. There is no question of a temptation against abandonment. Fr Libermann, who was one of the greatest spiritual masters of the 19th century, has left us many letters of direction. And he says more or less this: 'One of the things that paralyses most people in their relations with God and prevents them from advancing more, is the lack of confidence and hope.' And he adds that it is a point where the director will have to battle most energetically in order to know the quality of hope in the one he is directing, without stopping short at the 'problems and temptations' which are disturbing them.

The person who has not been tempted against hope, what does he/she know? I will say that in our day, it is the temptation which above all lies in wait for Christians. There is not so much a crisis of faith as there is of hope. The militants, the priests, ordinary Christians are tempted to give up and say: 'What can we do in this situation?' This is why the militants are disinterested in political or trade-union action and are interested in direct services, such as Mother Teresa does.

The person of greater faith is the one who has known these temptations against hope and has passed through them. The person of lesser faith has not known these temptations, which forge Christians and make them pass from infancy to adulthood. And do not look for 'tricks' — excuse the expression — to escape these temptations. I am thinking here of all those who say: 'There is no sin, no hell!' We have to struggle against every feeling of guilt, that is true, but not abandon real fear of God. One of the reasons that morality is in a state of crisis is that we refuse to acknowledge that we are sinners and fear God. Those who refuse to fear and to cry out to God are refusing at the same time the temptation against hope and are therefore excusing themselves from having confidence in merciful Love, as Thérèse says.

God is not some kind of indulgent simple-minded grandfather who passes the sponge over our stupidities. He has too much respect for our liberty to act in this way. We can only speak of mercy if we believe in justice and sanctity. And mercy is precisely that power which God has, to take a hardened heart, touch it and draw from it a cry which he cannot resist. It is confidence that makes us cry out to God. It is what justifies the boundless confidence that Thérèse preaches.

When a person does not send forth this cry of confidence to God, because he or she is fast asleep in the slumber of a false security, an abyss separates them from merciful Love. There are some whose consciences are perfectly tranquil because they have suppressed the demands of God in their lives. I must put you on your guard against all teaching that holds Thérèse's message of confidence as worthless. I do not want to frighten you, but rather encourage you by giving you the real security of the poor.

Thérèse's doctrine is addressed to those who would like to renounce themselves but who cannot achieve it. If you suffer because you do not love God and you humbly admit this, then Thérèse has a word for you. I am thinking here of Marie Noël's beautiful prayer for which Thérèse may have been responsible:

'My God, I do not love you, I do not even desire it. I am weary of you. Perhaps I do not even believe in you. But look on me in passing. Hide yourself for a moment in my soul, put it in order by a breath without my knowing it, without saying a word of it to me. If you want me to believe in you, give me faith. If you want me to love you, give me love. I do not have any and I can do nothing for it. I give you what I have: my weakness, my sorrow. And that tenderness which torments me and that you see so well ... And that despair ... And that crazy shame ... My pain, nothing but my pain ... And my hope! It is everything.'

Hope with Thérèse

If you have said Marie Noël's prayer, from the depths of your heart and not only with your lips, you are ready to listen to Thérèse's message about merciful Love. This message has been put into concrete langauge by Fr Desbuquois, a specialist on Thérèse from the years 1900-1920, in a book which has just been re-edited, *L'Esperance*.[1] Fr Desbuquois was a very involved man of action and the founder of Popular Action. If this book has been re-edited today it is because it answers a need of our age which is marked by a crisis of hope. What does Fr Desbuquois say?

Firstly he makes clear that Thérèse is addressing herself to souls less tempered than she. Thérèse's sisters have always said that strength was her characteristic. Some who read her writings run the risk of misunderstanding her and thinking that she is a 'fragile saint'. God certainly gave Thérèse extraordinary strength, but he also gave her the instinct to understand that what she was teaching did not presuppose the strength that she had. Mother Agnès confided: 'God gave her great sufferings so as to authenticate her message, but that does not mean that suffering is an integral part of her message.' The fourth section of *A Memoir of my Sister* is entitled 'Fortitude in Suffering'. Thérèse also said clearly to Céline and to Marie of the Trinity, concerning the act of offering to merciful Love: 'Indeed, in her mind there was no question of offering oneself to a whole train of supererogatory sufferings, but of abandoning oneself with complete confidence to God's Mercy' (ibid. 92).

Thérèse's message is addressed to the weak and not to the strong, but on the condition that they acknowledge their weakness and abandon themselves to God. Basically, Thérèse is speaking to those who, like Marie Noël, do not have her faith, her hope, or her charity. Secretly we react in the following way when someone speaks to us about sanctity and the love of God, and the unfortunate part is that we are

1 *L'Esperance*, P.G. Desbuquois, French edition, revised, presented by Pierre Bigo, SJ, and prepared by Andre Rayez, SJ, Beauchesne, 1978.

resigned to it. How many times have I heard this said: 'Sanctity is not for everyone!' The first fault against faith! Then they add: 'Sanctity, that's not for me!' And there is then a second fault against hope.

Thérèse wants to speak to those whose generosity wavers; who would like to renounce themselves, be healed and love God to the full measure of their vocation and who do not make it. Normally, what does one say to these people? Fr Desbuquois himself answers: 'Know how to will.' These words are written by a Jesuit whose educative preoccupation in the colleges is to teach how to will. Is not this how we were treated when we spoke of our difficulties? We were told: 'Make an effort! renounce yourself!' This seems very much to be the language of the Gospel: 'Renounce yourself, carry your cross!' It is what Cassian and all the spiritual masters say. There is no sanctity without renouncement: it is a matter of take it or leave it!

True sanctity

This is a language that risks being forgotten today when all doctrines and teaching, even the Gospels are 'toned down', by saying: 'God does not ask so much!' And this is serious, because with the same stroke we wipe out the whole of the Gospel and we no longer need Thérèse's message of confidence. I would like to cite here a text of Fr Guibert, the former editor of *Revue d'Ascetique et de Mystique* who is greatly interested in the lives of the saints. Each time that I read it, it makes a deep impression on my listeners:

'The work of self-abnegation is of the utmost importance in life. In fact, in the spiritual life it is almost the decisive point, the dominant strategic position which decides defeat or victory in the battle of sanctity.

'This is proved by experience: let us look at the lives of the unsuccessful saints, I mean those priests, religious or ordinary Christians who are excellent, fervent, zealous, pious and devoted, but who, nevertheless, are not saints.

'We look to see what is missing. It is not a deep interior life, nor a sincere love of God and of souls, but rather they lack a certain completeness in their renunciation, a certain depth of abnegation and total self-forgetfulness which would have surrendered them to God's work in them.

'To love God, to praise him, to tire oneself out, even to kill oneself in his service, so many things attract religious souls. But to die totally to self, obscurely in the silence of one's soul, to detach oneself, to let oneself be detached completely through grace, from all that is not the pure will of God, that is the secret holocaust before which most souls draw back. It is the precise point where their road forks between a fervent life and a life of high sanctity.'

There is a whole world of difference between a 'saintly man or woman' and a real 'saint'. The saintly person tries to circle round God by flying at a low altitude while the saint breaks the sound barrier. He or she has accepted to follow Christ and to renounce all. Let us note that it is not a question of performing ascetical feats, but as Fr Guibert says, of 'letting oneself be detached completely by God'. This is the language of the Gospel and no one coming into contact with it can deny it: *We must never seek ourselves in anything whatsoever.* We know Christ's love in so far as we renounce ourselves. The same is true for our love of others: a person filled with self-love cannot love others.

If we cheat in this, we do not need Thérèse's message, for her doctrine is addressed precisely to those who are not able to make it, those of whom Christ was thinking when he said: *Come to me, all you who labour beneath the weight of the burden* (Mt 2:28). Christ addresses himself to those who are weary and who can no longer try to keep the law and who do not succeed, not those who are resting. It is necessary to try and to will. Thérèse's message is addressed to those who acknowledge that they must renounce themselves but who do not succeed in doing so. It is a practical problem: *I fail to carry out the things I want to do* (Rom 7:15).

Faced with this practical impossibility, there is the temptation to say: 'I cannot' and that involves a twofold truth, says Fr Molinié, who has inspired us very much in this work. The two truths are:
1. I cannot; and
2. I will not.

And the astuteness of the demon is to mix these two truths. – If we do not want to, we are free and no one can make us. If we refuse, it is God's judgment and in the end punishment. – If we cannot, Thérèse answers us: *If the most imperfect souls understand this, they would have no fear.* What is impossible for us is possible for God. He is infinite and to make it possible for us, he sends us the strength of the Holy Spirit. Spiritual astuteness is not to mix the two.

I would now like to give you Thérèse's answer interpreted by Fr Desbuquois. When you do not succeed in renouncing yourself in some area, for example anger, impurity or intemperance, it is necessary to try just the same, knowing that it is not a matter of succeeding or not succeeding. With Thérèse, the line is drawn between those who try and those who do not try. Between two persons with the same results, there can be an abyss: there are those who want to renounce themselves and who are not able and there are those who manage to be tranquil. In spite of being confronted with the sight of their weakness, they blunt their sensitivity. 'God does not ask so much!' they say, or worse still, they put to death in them all sense of sin.

143

The first will come to know the temptation against hope and this will be their salvation. They will be driven to cry out: 'Help', and receive from God a magnificent response. If they turn aside from this temptation, they will be turning away at the same time from what will give them salvation and sanctity. In one sense, the temptation will be their means of crying to God and therefore of being united to him. It will enable them to realise Jesus' word: *Pray without ceasing, without ever being discouraged* (Lk 18:1). On this subject John Climacus says: 'Do not say, after having persevered in prayer for a long time, that you have achieved nothing; for you have already obtained the result. What greater good, in fact, than to be attached to the Lord and to persevere firmly in that union with him.'

The most serious danger that we encounter here is in avoiding this temptation, to be discouraged or to turn away from it. We do not mean the temptation against generosity, but the temptation against hope and confidence which we find in the *Our Father* and this is why we say to God: *Lead us not into temptation*! How does this temptation come into play? We will see that in the next chapter.

12

At the foot of the stairs

We left the aspirant to sanctity at grips with the temptation against hope and confidence. Today let us look at how this temptation comes into play. This is how Fr Desbuquois explains Thérèse's answer: *Keep trying, do not become discouraged! But beware, the more you try, the more discouraged you will be.* The first solution consists in suppressing the effort and then there is peace.

The second solution is that of the Gospel: *Become once again a little child that expects everything from its Father.* The problem is basically that the Gospel has been badly misunderstood, the Sermon on the Mount has been interpreted as a moral code: to forgive one's enemies, to offer the right cheek to someone who has struck you on the left, not to lust after a woman in one's heart ... So many things which are impossible for us men and women. Christ has asked this of us precisely in order to make us understand that we are incapable of them, after we have tried to achieve them. For only then can he say to us: *Unless you become again as a little child ...* (Mt 18:3). And *what is impossible for man and woman is possible for God* (Mt 19:26). Note that this word of Jesus follows immediately after the apostles' reflection on the impossibility of perfect chastity. For it is only then that he can give us his love so that we can love the Father and do his will with all our heart. *If I am to love you*, Thérèse says, *you must lend me your own heart.*

Thérèse will only be repeating the Gospel when she says to us: *Keep trying, make yourselves little and humble as a child, look at God's heart and hope from his love the grace to love him and hope against hope for the grace to renounce what is not he!* Thérèse's way is not an easy way for it never foregoes the equation: to love God equals renouncing what is not God. St Augustine said that we must love God and despise self or love self and despise God.

To enter into this perspective, we have to be mad enough to hope to obtain what we cannot bring about ourselves, yet to do what we can to remain little. Thérèse says to Sr Marie of the Trinity: *The only way to make rapid progress in the way of love is to remain always very little, this is what I have done; so now I can sing with St John of the Cross:*

> *And as I sank so low, so low,*
> *So high, so high, did upward go,*
> *That in the end I reached my prey.*

In reality, Thérèse's little way is none other than the 'narrow way' of St John of the Cross and it is necessary to be very little to enter upon it: 'I still hear her saying to me with her inimitable accent, and with her gracious gestures: *And as I sank so low, so low,* etc. (Sr Marie of the Trinity)

'To lift her little foot'

Thérèse has described a gymnastic feat in a gripping and thought-provoking image which she made use of for Sr Marie of the Trinity who was passing through a temptation against hope. Thérèse was demanding with her novices and would not allow anything to be passed over by them. Thérèse said to the novice who was discouraged by her imperfections and her apparently futile efforts:

You remind me of a very little child who is beginning to stand up, but does not yet know how to walk. Determined to reach the top of the stairs to find its mother, it lifts its little foot so as to climb up to the first step. Wasted effort! It keeps falling back without being able to go on.

Thérèse accepts the starting point: the child cannot climb up even onto the first step, but it lifts its foot.

Ah! then, be this little child, by practising all the virtues, keep lifting your little foot to climb the stairs of sanctity, and do not think that you will be able to get up even to the first step. No; but God asks only for your good will. 'Thérèse had a beautiful expression for this *good will*; she said it was a *'little dog who saves us from all dangers and which no one can resist'* (CSG).

To the realist this is absurd! There is no need to try and climb up, there is but one thing to be occupied with, but above all beware of trying to love God. Thérèse says: 'If you have faith, know that from the top of the stairs, God is watching you and he is waiting':

At the top of these stairs, he (God) is looking at you lovingly. Soon conquered by your vain efforts, he will come down himself, and, taking you in his arms, will carry you forever into his Kingdom where you will not leave him again. But if you stop lifting your little foot, he will leave you on earth for a long time.

It would be absurd to try and climb the stairs if God were not at the top, watching and waiting for us. And when he judges that we are ripe enough, in the right condition — and this is the paradox — for this apparently fruitless and futile effort produces a result: it wears out our pretentions, our hardness and our pride, so as to make us pliable and docile. This is why the saints undertook macerations (think how one has to macerate gherkins in vinegar!). 'What is the

147

purpose of fasts and vigils?' an old man asked Abba Moïse; he replied: 'They have no other purpose but to make a person completely humble. If this fruit is produced in the soul, God's heart is moved in his/her regard.' The person's heart is 'like dried hay' and when he/she has 'almost given in to all temptations', God can intervene and send 'the holy strength' needed to conquer the passions (St Macarius). Then God will come for us and take us to the top of the stairs.

Thérèse's doctrine is addressed to those who are tempted against hope and are not trying any other solution. Then the door opens and God takes us up. Sr Marie of the Trinity will say: 'From that day, I was no longer distressed at seeing myself always at the foot of the stairs. Knowing my powerlessness to lift myself even one step, I let the others go up and I am happy to keep on lifting up my little foot by continued efforts. I am therefore awaiting in peace that blessed day when Jesus will come down himself to carry me up in his arms.'

At that moment, Thérèse said to me, *will you be further advanced for having climbed five or six steps through your own strength? Is it more difficult for Jesus to take you from the bottom rather than from half way up the stairs?*

And Thérèse is going to give the profound reason for her advice, which looks beyond the result and aims above all at making us humble and wearing away our pretentions to lay hold of God: *There is another benefit of not being able to go up and it is that you always remain humble. If your own efforts were crowned with success, you would not arouse Jesus' compassion, he would leave you to climb all alone and there would be every reason to fear that you would fall into self-complacency.* (Sr Marie of the Trinity)

We have to make a concrete effort in our own life. We try to struggle against a temptation and achieve nothing. What

148

remains for us to do? To go on simply, trying to believe and to hope that merciful Love is waiting for us at the end of our difficult efforts and he will come for us. If we do that, God will give us the grace of Love and in so far as it increases in us, so too will the spirit of sacrifice increase. And this is still her doctrine: we do not reach love through the spirit of sacrifice, but we reach the spirit of sacrifice through love. And how do we attain this Love? It is Thérèse again who answers us: *It is confidence and nothing but confidence that leads to Love.*

'The further you advance, the fewer struggles you will have' (CSG)

Thérèse does not give any receipt and she does not promise Sr Marie of the Trinity that she will not have to struggle any more, but she wants to put effort in its right place. It will still be necessary to struggle, but not in the sense that we understand it. At all costs we must avoid what we call the 'fight'. This is the worst struggle inspired by pride. In the beginning, the novice struggles unskillfully in fruitless combat, doomed to failure, like the combat of St Peter who wanted to follow Jesus to death. There is a first phase where Peter tries to be faithful to Jesus Christ through his own strength. At a given moment, when Jesus looks at him after his betrayal, he breaks down in tears. Now he will be able to lead the real battle. *I have fought the good fight. I have finished my course, I have kept the faith* (2 Tim 4:7). Paul relied more on the grace of God than on his own strength and his deeds (2 Tim 1:9). It is the example of Blessed Suso recounted by Thérèse.

A very profound and a very penetrating light is needed in order to discern the right struggle from the wrong. We have to desire this light and ask for it so as to fight the true fight. Thérèse will say at the end of her life to her sister Céline: *The further you advance, the fewer struggles you will have, or rather you will overcome them more easily, because you will see the right side of things. Then your soul will rise above creatures* (CSG). St Benedict says more or less the same thing in the Prologue of his Rule: 'As one makes progress in the monastic life and grows in faith, the heart is dilated, and runs the way of divine teachings with an inexpressible sweetness of love.'

Thérèse will often say to her sisters that they have to struggle against this philosophy which says: 'Life is hard', and admit secretly: 'God is hard'. How many hold a grudge against God and will not forgive him for creating them! This is blasphemy, for we are the ones who are hard. Someone said to Thérèse: 'Life is sad.' *No*, she replied, *exile is sad, but life is joy.*

It is hard enough for God, she said, *who loves us so much to have to leave us on earth to fulfil our time of trial, without us continually coming to him and reminding him that we are sick of it. We should act as if we did not notice it ... suffer on the sly, as it were, so as not to give God time to see it* (CSG).

We must struggle while saying: 'Lord Jesus, have mercy on me. I know that I cannot come through this on my own, that it is the result of my pride and my hidden imperfections, but it is not your fault!' Then when we accept to judge ourselves before him, God can clothe us with his mercy. At that moment, he sends us a grace, as he did to Thérèse on 9 June 1895 when she discovered merciful Love and offered herself to it. The life of the saints was a struggle, but they struggled against hardness of heart in order to have confidence and call out 'help'! There is one problem and one difficulty in life: to know how to call to God. It is the real struggle, that of unprofitable servants who sing of their love and beseech God.

'I was lamenting the fact that God seemed to have abandoned me ...' Sr Thérèse quickly replied: *Oh! no, do not say that! You know that when I do not understand what is happening, I smile, I say 'Thank you', I appear always happy before God. We must not doubt him, that would be disloyalty. No, never any 'imprecations' against Providence, but always gratitude* (CSG).

To conclude, let us say finally that the attitude Thérèse recommended to Sr Marie of the Trinity can also help us to see clearly in the debate which sometimes opposes the moral life or spirituality and the psyche. It is not always easy to disentangle our own personal responsibility for our weaknesses and falls. An impaired psyche, not to say an unbalanced psyche, can cause a person to fail when his/her spiritual liberty remains intact. Often, a person seems to put a check on God at his/her obvious conscious level, when in the depths of the heart, that person is consenting to God. Thérèse understood this very well: *It is a great trial to see everything black, but it does not depend on you completely* (LT 241).

But attention is also needed, for the plan of liberty is sometimes involved, without our knowing it, in that of the psyche. It is possible that if we are not directly responsible for this weakness, we are responsible for it in another domain where we are not conscious of it. In the liturgy we often ask God to: 'Purify us from our hidden faults!' The easiest thing to do then is not to attempt to discern our own responsibilities, but to confess our misery humbly, without knowing it and ask God to reveal it to us:

When you are not practising virtue you must not blame it on some natural cause, such as ill-health, the weather, or some trial. You should make it a means of growing in humility and count yourself among the little souls, since you are so weak in practising virtue. What you need now, is not to practise heroic virtue, but to acquire humility. For this end, there will always be some imperfections in your victories, so that you will not dwell on them with satisfaction. Rather, you will be humbled when you recall them for they will remind you that you are not a great soul. There are some souls who, as long as they are on this earth, never have the joy of seeing themselves appreciated by creatures. This keeps them from thinking that they possess the virtue they admire in others (CSG).

Conclusion: Why are you troubled?

I would like to leave you with one word, perhaps the most profound in the Gospel, which is frequently on Christ's lips when he speaks to his apostles and disciples: *Do not fear! Do not be afraid, little flock! Why are you troubled?* And then, when he had quelled the storm and had calmed their fear, he added this word which should suffice to pacify us: *Take heart, it is I, have no fear* (Mk 6:50).

Basically, we are afraid because we are alone, but the day we discover the gaze which is attentive and full of the Father's tenderness, fear is replaced by abandonment. It is not a complacent optimism but a confidence based on God's efficacious love.

Thérèse says so often: it does not depend on us whether we see life through rose-coloured or dark glasses. Fear and anxiety are deeply rooted in us and we have to go back to the way of spiritual childhood to understand that we have been 'scorching along' (to use a beautifully vivid expression) in fear and tension. We have to see clearly that this is the starting point and to accept it, then we can take it up and come out from it.

Too often, we flee because this awareness would reveal to us the truth that we are creatures dependent on the Father's love. So we experience the need to reassure ourselves by fleeing from it. It is a great secret to sound the depths of our fear, to abandon ourselves to it, crying out for help. I know some men and women who have very fearful temperaments and who, by letting themselves plummet to the depths of their fear, have thereby fallen into God. They had the courage to be afraid and to cry out: 'My God, mercy!'

The greater the fear that we have the courage to face, the greater still will be our experience of God. For we will then have found the only attitude valid for reuniting us with God, the cry to him which gives way to abandonment: *Father, into your hands I commend my spirit!*

For that, we must live by grace, in the present moment and above all, says Thérèse, not store up provisions. We have to abandon the past to God's mercy and entrust the future to his Providence. St John of the Cross says that this supposes a purification of the memory, I would say of that faculty which has the power to arouse fears and terrors in us by recalling past memories. Imaginary sufferings are always unbearable and, usually they never come to pass.

You can imagine the trial that you will have in an hour or tomorrow, says Fr Molinié, but you cannot imagine the grace that you will be given at that moment. Woe betide you if you rely more on your own strength than on the grace. St Benedict often says that the monk falls because he presumed God's grace. The psychologists tells us that if a person's memory could be suppressed, their suffering would immediately be suppressed. Faced with an actual trial, we must then rely only on the grace of the moment, by making an act of confidence each time.

We wish to stop at this word of Thérèse. It sums up very well all that we have tried to say about hope as well as abandonment. To a novice who was expressing her fears for the future, Thérèse said something like this: *To busy oneself with the future is to meddle in creation and to take God's place.*

13

'To please God'

We have followed Thérèse along *the road that leads to love, the way of abandonment* (Ms B 188). We have tried to situate this road in its spiritual geography and above all we have shown the topography with its bends and its windings, so that anyone who enters upon it might know where they are placing their steps. It is now time to conclude, to return to Thérèse's fundamental intuition, for the route is made to pass along and not to stay on. And this intuition is love! You might say to me that this is nothing new since love is the very basis of the Gospel and therefore of sanctity.

But there is something original about Thérèse and we have noted this in the last chapters. With Thérèse, one does not attain love through the spirit of sacrifice, but rather reaches the spirit of sacrifice through love. And indeed, we come to love through confidence and nothing but confidence! This is the way of the Gospel. Her sister Céline noted clearly the originality of Thérèse's message: love of God is not only the end of the way but also its source. Love impelled her to act.

'Unlike other mystics who strove after perfection to attain love, St Thérèse of the Child Jesus took as her way the perfection of love itself. Love was the object of her whole life, the moving force behind all her actions' (CSG).

'I work for his pleasure'

And with her, love will take a form of gratuitousness and discretion which has as its only goal to give joy to God. This is why she will use an expression which recurs often in her writings and in those of her sisters: *To please God*. She will say to Mother Marie de Gonzague: *What she (your child) esteems, what she desires is only to please Jesus* (Ms C 208). We hesitate a little to use this phrase because it has lost its meaning through the finical usage that has been made of it. At every turn, certain people had it on their lips, especially when they wanted to obtain a sacrifice from another, they would say: 'Make this effort to please God'. It was also used as a motive for a 'rose-water' spirituality. The word 'pleasure' is not so acceptable today because the human sciences have associated it with inferior and gross satisfactions and so we have people speaking about a pleasure ethic. And yet I do not think we should refrain from using it since Thérèse used it and for her it meant a veritable spiritual attitude. Perhaps it would be more precise to say 'to give joy to God' rather than 'to please God'.[1] I am thinking of that eight-year-old child to whom someone was speaking about a religious who was celebrating her silver jubilee, and who said of her: 'She has given joy to God.' This word 'joy' has a more gratuitous and a more spiritual connotation.

But let us return to Thérèse's expression to see the spiritual attitude she drew from it, it is always the same. 'During her illness she confided to me: *I have only ever desired to please God. I have never sought to amass merits, otherwise, now I would be despairing* (CSG). She knows that our best deeds are tarnished before God, and 'in her humility, she regarded

---

1 In French the same word 'plaisir' (pleasure) is also used in the expression 'faire plaisir' (to please someone). The point the author is making is lost in the English translation (Trans. note).

as worthless the works she had done and esteemed only the love which had inspired them' (ibid.).

A similar attitude should be ours when we give someone a present. The only reason for our gesture should be to please, to give joy, and if a smile lights up the person's face, that would be our best reward. Jesus will come back repeatedly in the Sermon on the Mount to this gratuitous love for others: *If you love those who love you, what credit is that to you? Even sinners love those who love them ... And if you lend to those from whom you hope a return, what credit is that to you? Even sinners lend to sinners so that they will receive the same back in return. But love your enemies, do good and lend to those from whom there is no hope of a return* (Lk 6:32-35).

Basically, Thérèse reacts very strongly against a utilitarian and mercantile type spirituality that seeks to acquire merits in return for what is done for God. We *are not justified by good works, nor by practising the Law, but through faith in Jesus Christ* (Gal 2:16). One day I met a young Cistercian who had been converted after a rather exciting life and who said something similar to Thérèse: 'How can you do something for God without his knowing it?'

The great Saints worked for the glory of God, but I am only a little soul, I will work for his pleasure, for his 'fancies' and I would be happy to bear the greatest sufferings, even, if it were possible, without his knowing it, not for any passing glory he might derive from them — that would be too beautiful — but simply to make him smile, even once ... There are so many who want to be useful! My dream is to be a little toy in the hand of the Infant Jesus ... I am a 'whim' of the little Jesus (CSG).

Thérèse's dream, to be 'unpetalled' is to proclaim that God alone is important and that we are useless: 'It suffices that we want to be useless', she says! This is also what the Blessed

Virgin proclaims in the Magnificat for she knows that God's gifts are gratuitous. Thérèse rejoices and thanks God for all his gifts to her. She gives thanks that she is so precious in God's sight while being useless. This is why she dreams of being unpetalled and of pouring out her strength in libation, that is to say, for nothing: only to please God. She will say to her sister Céline who envied her works and would have dearly loved to write poetry: *We must not set our hearts on that ... Oh! no, when we are confronted by our limitations, we must offer up the works of others, that is the benefit of belonging to the Communion of Saints. You must never grieve over it, but apply yourself solely to loving* (CSG).

'Not allowing one little sacrifice to escape'

This word is completely Thérèse: *You must apply yourself solely to loving.* And on another occasion, she will say: *Our only duty is to be united with God* (CSG). But with her, love has nothing to do with pious resolutions, it is translated into deeds. It is an effective love, such as Christ commands in the Gospel: *It is not those who say Lord, Lord who shall enter the Kingdom, but those who do the will of my Father in heaven.* Ignatius of Loyola will say the same thing in the Contemplation to obtain love, which could be compared to the act of Offering to merciful Love: 'Love must be put more into deeds than into words' (*Exercises* 230).

Thérèse always connects love with the effective gift of herself which goes beyond the little acts. While she is detached from great spectacular acts and works of penance which flatter pride, she holds on to the little acts done through love. For this is obedience to the promptings of the Spirit which sends us back to obedience to Christ and to the Church. Christ tells us that it will be of no use to us to have kept all the commandments if we have not obeyed the Spirit. He will say to the rich young man: 'One thing you still lack' (Lk 18:22): simply to have answered his gratuitous invitation and left all. For Thérèse, to be un-petalled, to be consumed, to burn in God's flame is to show her love through little sacrifices. The word is outdated and yet it is of great importance, even if it does cause a smile today.

A teacher said to me one day: 'Formerly much was said about sacrifices and very little of love. Today much is said about love and very little about sacrifice.' This is true! We have all been formed with the idea that we had to make 'little sacrifices' to show our love for the Lord. We even kept an account of them. But there was the danger in this of a certain pharisaism and, above all of thinking that sanctity was the work of our own industry. Life then immediately proceeded to undeceive us and to show us, as it showed Thérèse, that God alone can make us saints. But today there needs to be a review of our understanding of sacrifice. Let us hear what Thérèse has to say about this:

> Yes, my Beloved, this is how my life will be consumed ... I have no other means of showing you my love than by throwing flowers, that is, of not allowing one little sacrifice to escape, not one look, not one word, but by profiting from all the smallest things and doing them out of love ... I want to suffer for love and even to rejoice for love so that in this way I will throw flowers before your throne. I shall not come upon one without unpetalling it for you ... Then while I am throwing my flowers, I shall sing (for could one cry when doing such a joyous thing?) I will sing, even when I have to gather my flowers in the midst of thorns, and my song will be all the more melodious when the thorns are longest (Ms B 196).

What does Thérèse mean when she speaks of 'little sacrifices' 'to please God'? She knows very well that one cannot love Christ without renouncing self. Then since she is incapable of doing great things, she must be glad that she can do little things, and for the sole aim of proclaiming her love, and above all her obedience to Christ. We know how Thérèse dreamed of performing great penances and how she found herself to be incapable of them. It is humiliating to desire the infinite and to be limited by one's physical reality.

Mother Marie de Gonzague had told her to use a foot-warmer in winter to keep her feet warm. And Thérèse said humorously: *Others will go into heaven with their instruments of penance and I will have my foot-warmer, but it is love and obedience alone which count* (CSG). She held obedience above all else and taught her novices not to be negligent in this matter, especially with regard to asking for little permissions and she admitted that these *trifles were a martyrdom* (ibid.).

We could be tempted to smile at these 'little sacrifices' and yet they are of the utmost importance for those who are following Christ in the way of spiritual childhood. We may smile, but let us be honest: are we capable of great things? So if you feel that you cannot practise heroic obedience in big things – God will ask them of you later, as Jesus said to Peter: 'Another will gird you and carry you where you do not wish to go' – and imitate Jesus in his agony, proclaim your desire through acts which, in themselves, count for nothing but this proclamation.

To smile, to set in order matters which are dragging along, to accept a humiliation in silence, to close a door, to write a letter you have been putting off, to pray for an extra quarter of an hour, to render a service ... actions which have no outward manifestation and which, in themselves do not make you advance in the spiritual life, but which proclaim your powerlessness to walk towards God yourself. This simple proclamation, by the very fact that it is obeying an inspiration of the Spirit, is a poor and an easy obedience. And it is precisely because it is easy that it is difficult, for we always like to do spectacular things so as to acquire for ourselves a sanctity by dint of our own efforts.

I can only offer very little things'

Thérèse did not cease repeating to Céline and to the novices: do not worry about your work, that is not important, but rather the love that animates your life: *Go to your little duty* she said to her sister, *not to your little love.* Love to do hidden things, with the sole aim of giving joy to God alone and of saving souls: *What a mystery it is! We can help missionaries and convert souls far away through our practice of virtue and hidden acts of charity* (CSG). Whether she prayed, gave alms or fasted, Thérèse hid these acts from others and did them only beneath the gaze of the Father who sees in secret. She hid what was best in her, so that God alone might take joy in it and others might profit best from it.

In this sense Thérèse was truly chaste: *The Holy Virgin,* she says, *was careful to keep everything to herself, no one could begrudge me for doing the same.* 'Chastity,' says Fr Molinié, 'is the joy of belonging to God. This joy inspires in us the need to hide ourselves so that we might belong to him and he might be the only one to rejoice over us: only to reveal ourselves to others to the degree that he himself asks. The spirit of chastity is therefore a soul of silence. Any useless revelation of ourselves is already something impure.'

Untiringly, Thérèse returns to these little sacrifices of which daily life is woven. And when we experience weakness and the inability to do these little things, we must rejoice in our poverty. Sr Geneviève said to her: 'You are so sensitive to God and I am not, I would so much like to be like that! Perhaps my desire for it suffices?'

Indeed, especially if you accept the humiliation of it. If you can rejoice over it that will please Jesus more than if you had never been lacking in sensitivity, and say: *My God, I thank you that I have not had one sensitive feeling and I rejoice to see it in others ... You fill me with joy, Lord, when I see all that you do* (CSG). Fr Bro entitled one of his Lenten conferences at Notre Dame, 'Thank God that you are without hope!'

We ought to reread here the book *A Memoir of my Sister* and see precisely how Thérèse reacted and lived love in the midst of the most ordinary actions of daily life. She expresses it very well to Mother Marie de Gonzague in her Manuscript: *My dear Mother, you see that I am a very little soul who can offer God only very little things, still it often happens that I allow some of these little sacrifices which give such peace to my soul to escape me; but this does not discourage me, I put up with having a little less peace and try to be more vigilant on another occasion* (Ms C 250).

Thérèse sets down therefore lowly acts, not physically difficult, but which show her will and her joy in not acting on her own accord. *When we renounce self, we have our reward on earth. You often ask me how one can attain pure love: forget self and do not seek yourself in anything* (CSG).

We go after difficult things because we are looking for a certain glamour that comes from having made an effort ourselves. That is not it. The easier the act is, the truer it is from the point of view of obedience. 'She told me simply that, in unimportant matters she had made a habit of obeying everybody, in a spirit of faith, as if it were God himself manifesting his will to her' (CSG). It is the purest act of love that we can do, Thérèse tells us.

In our spiritual life, we can find many excuses for our failings due to weakness: to lose our temper, for example. There are some faults that are practically unavoidable. But on the other hand, there are some sins for which we do not have any excuse, except it be from sheer pride. We can always pray, for example, do without something at a meal, avoid saying a word which would add fuel to the fire: this is what Christ is asking, very simple things that are within our reach and that we can do without any excuse. You should read the pages on the experience of grace in everyday life by Karl Rahner, *(Vivre et croire aujourd'hui)*. He shows how the Christian experiences the life of the Trinity within him to the extent that he abandons himself freely to God in the everyday realities of life. It cites very simple examples: to remain alone in a room to pray, to forgive someone without being compelled by any other motive except that of obeying Christ who asks that we forgive our enemies.

To really wake up to God's love

When we really wake up to God's love, we begin to realise that things have to change in our life and that we have to be converted. We stumble along in so many areas and we have to get the better of so many faults. We do not have the faith to pull down those mountains of egotism and cast them into the sea. We do not have the faith of the Canaanite woman which was so great, but we can ask Christ for faith like a mustard seed which already, nevertheless, shifts mountains a little.

The drama is that we want to change ourselves all at once, so we dream up shattering resolutions about prayer, service or asceticism, more imaginary than real and which we quickly forget all about the next day because of our weakness, but they do help calm our conscience. The Lord does not ask us to undertake all that at once, but to do what we can today, in joy and in peace, because we know that it is good for us.

This is the meaning of the little sacrifices Thérèse asks for in the movement of abandonment. Usually, there is a zone in our heart where God is specially calling us to conversion which is always the beginning of a new life.

There is a corner in us where he is nudging us and reminding us that, if we are serious with him, there must be change. Often it is the point we would like to forget and perhaps take up later. We do not want to listen to his word condemning us for this and, consequently, we try to forget it and distract ourselves by working in some other safer corner, which needs changing, but not with the same prick of conscience.

This is where Thérèse invites us to live abandonment. It is not easy to recognise in ourselves this precise zone where God is calling us to conversion. We blunt our perception by working on another point that we want to correct, when the Lord precisely wants the other. Thérèse taught her novices to feel and recognise the call to conversion that God is addressing to them concerning such a zone in their life. She did it in a very simple way when her sisters came to tell her about the difficulties they were experiencing at each present moment. If they are stumbling over such a particular point it is because God is at work in them in this area and waiting for them there today. They should therefore work with him and help him by making positive acts, rather than by arbitrarily attacking this or that imperfection.

Gradually, we will come through these little acts to a personal experience of the love that the Lord has for us and we will abandon ourselves to him. Abandonment passes also through this concrete form of renouncement. Examine yourself here: by not refusing to accept these acts of pure love, without glamour, without show, just as Christ had no other glory than that of not doing his own will ... This is how you will become saints and will be happy:

'You should never seek yourself in anything whatsoever for as soon as you begin to seek self, at that moment, you cease loving (*Imitation* Bk 111, 5,7). *At the end of my religious life, I am leading the happiest life that one could have, because I never sought myself* (CSG).

And the last word with which I would like to leave you at the end of this work is this: only those who avoid being evil and teach others not to become evil are happy people. But let us not forget either that only those who have found intimacy with Christ are truly blessed.

Conclusion

'My vocation is love'

At the end of these pages, perhaps we have gained an insight into Thérèse's mission as set forth in the Introduction and which is to make Love loved or rather, as she herself expressed it in the act of offering: *O my God! Blessed Trinity, I desire to love you and to make you loved* (Clarke 276). In concluding, I invite you to read or to reread the Letter to Sr Marie of the Sacred Heart commonly called Manuscript B, a veritable theological exposition of Theresian spirituality, where Thérèse gives her sister Marie *a souvenir of her retreat* which she made at the beginning of September 1896 and of which we have already spoken (Chapter 5: *Confidence and nothing but confidence*). Thérèse had received great lights as to her vocation during this retreat, and so on 13 September, Sr Marie of the Sacred Heart, her eldest sister, asked her to put them in writing. Thérèse wrote these pages between 13 and 16 September 1896.

We will not discuss again the textual problems which we have already analysed, but the conclusion where Thérèse says that she has discovered her vocation at the end of a long road which is recalled in this chapter: *Then, in the excess of my delirious joy, I cried out: 'O Jesus, my Love ... at last I have found my vocation ... MY VOCATION IS LOVE'* (Ms B 194). And Thérèse herself writes this concise formula in capital letters.

One is almost tempted to say with a smile: 'You therefore needed eight years, after you entered Carmel, to discover your vocation!' No, she was not satisfied with being a Carmelite, Christ's spouse and mother of souls in order to realise fully the special name the Father had given her when he created her. That name which we shall all bear written in us, *engraved on a white stone and which no one will know except the one who receives it* (Rev 2:17). We spend our whole life searching to find this name: we do not know it, we only know we need it, as Lewis says: 'it has never really taken shape in any thought, image or emotion. It is always calling us out of ourselves to follow it and if we stay seated ruminating over this desire, and try to hold on to it, the desire itself escapes us' (Lewis, *The Problem of Suffering*).

Eight years were not too long for Thérèse to discover her vocation, for it did not fall on her from the heavens. Long before she entered Carmel, God's love had laid siege to her heart. From 25 December 1886 when she *felt charity enter into her heart and the need to forget self so as to please others* (Ms A 99), until 9 June 1894 when, offering herself to Merciful Love, she felt that Love was *penetrating, surrounding her, renewing and purifying her soul* (Ms A 181), there had been that whole discovery of her poverty and her nothingness, in a word, her misery, which had made her *fit for the workings of Love.*

It is usually said that she discovered her vocation to Love while she was reading chapters 12 and 13 of Paul's first letter to the Corinthians. A closer look shows that this is not correct since she herself says that she was not at peace:

> *At prayer, my desires made me suffer a veritable martyrdom, and I opened the letters of St Paul to look for some kind of answer. My eyes fell on chapters 12 and 13 of the first letter to the Corinthians. I read there, in the first chapter, that all cannot be apostles, prophets, doctors etc. ... that the Church is made up of different members, and that the eye cannot*

be the hand at one and the same time ... The answer was clear, but it did not satisfy my desires, it did not bring me peace (Ms B 193).

The answer is clear, but it does not satisfy Thérèse's desires. St Paul would have been a means that led her towards the discovery of her vocation, but this can only be revealed to her by the light of the Holy Spirit. And the Spirit will act in her through the gift of knowledge and it is his mission to make her discover 'the charm of being a creature' through the awareness of her 'nothingness'. In the ontological meaning of the term: she is a creature that receives its being from God. As we said above, this is the discovery that will hollow out in Thérèse the capacity to welcome Love and to discover her name. And so she continues: *Just as Mary Magdalene found what she was looking for by stooping down lower near the empty tomb, so I, by abasing myself to the depths of my nothingness, rose up so high that I was able to reach my goal* (Ms B 194). Then she will be able to hear the rest of Paul's word, but the Spirit had to dig down deeply enough in her so that God's Word, coming from outside, might fill her.

Without being discouraged I continued my reading and this sentence consoled me: 'Strive after the most perfect gifts.' And the apostle explains how all the most perfect gifts are nothing without love ... that Charity is the EXCELLENT WAY that leads most surely to God (Ms B ibid.).

Love, the Holy Spirit in person, will give Thérèse the key to her vocation, through the letter to the Corinthians, of course, but not by following the traditional schema of the members described by St Paul. This is where Thérèse is truly original in her discovery, for while integrating the doctrine of the members, she will go much further and place herself right in the heart of the Church. Her role was not to evangelise, nor teach, nor undergo martyrdom, but to interiorise Love in the heart of the Church in order to

169

sanctify it from within, just as the heart propels the blood through the whole body. She is not the one who sanctifies the Church, for this mission always comes back to the Holy Spirit, like the mission to evangelise, to prophesy or to catechise. Her mission is to offer herself to Love so that it might take possession of her and transform her. At last she has found rest, even if Love will keep her on the move until the day of her death and after that, since she will continue her mission in heaven. We should be open to this text which is the source of Thérèse's vocation, in prayer, for it could set free in us an interior word which might truly reveal to us our vocation, even if our vocation is closer to one described by St Paul in the members of the Body:

> At last I could rest ... Considering the mystical body of the Church, I had not recognised myself in any of the members described by St Paul, or rather I wanted to see myself in all of them ... Charity gave me the key to my vocation. I understood that if the Church had a body made up of different members, the most necessary, the most noble of all could not be missing, I understood that the Church had a heart, and that this heart was BURNING WITH LOVE. I understood that Love alone made the members act, and that if Love ever became extinct, the Apostles would not preach the Gospel, the Martyrs would refuse to shed their blood ... I understood that LOVE INCLUDED ALL VOCATIONS, THAT LOVE WAS EVERYTHING, THAT IT EMBRACED ALL TIMES AND ALL PLACES ... IN A WORD, THAT IT IS ETERNAL! (Ms B 194).

And it is here that she cries out: *My vocation is love.* She then immediately states specifically that this vocation has been given her by God, but that he had put the ardent desire for it into her heart. God does not give something without first giving the desire for it. A vocation does not fall from the heavens like a meteorite, but it is put in the person's desires: *Yes, I have found my place in the Church and this place,*

O my God, you have given to me ... in the heart of the Church, my Mother, I will be Love ... thus I shall be everything ... and my dream will be realised!!! ... (Ms B 194).

But the Love Thérèse will incarnate in the heart of the Church is not any Love, it is merciful Love. It is not a love which lifts itself up by its own sheer strength and which one can take hold of, it is a Love that humbles itself to the nothingness of the creature: *Yes, in order that Love be fully satisfied, it has to lower itself, it has to lower itself to nothingness so that it can transform this nothingness into fire* (Ms B 195).

In our relations with God, everything can be the occasion for us to become proud, even our desires for sanctity, asceticism and prayer and there is only one attitude of ours which cannot imitate or copy Love: to experience our weakness and poverty, to 'love it with sweetness', in a word to have a heart broken with sorrow, as Thérèse will say at the end of her autobiography: In manuscript B, she clearly expresses her thought:

I understood that my desires of being everything, of embracing all vocations, were riches that could render me unjust, so I made use of them to make friends. Remembering Eliseus' prayer to his Father Elijah when he dared ask him for his DOUBLE SPIRIT, I presented myself before the angels and saints and I said to them: 'I am the smallest of creatures, I know my misery and my weakness, but I also know how much noble and generous hearts love to do Good, I beg you then, O Blessed Inhabitants of heaven, I beg you to adopt me as your child, you alone will have the Glory which you will make me merit, but deign to answer my prayer, it is bold, I know, yet I dare to ask you to obtain for me YOUR TWOFOLD SPIRIT' (Ms B 195,6).

If it is gratuitous, welcomed and received, Love is not with Thérèse sheer sentiment, it is also effective and is shown through works. Only Thérèse knows that she cannot produce

171

brilliant works by which she would merit to obtain love, for her will is weak and she is poor on all levels, so she has but one solution: to respond to this love of God by means of all the little acts — which she calls 'little sacrifices' — whose sole *raison d'etre* is to confess that she is incapable of doing greater. There would be no excuse for her not performing these little sacrifices.

But how will this child show her love, since love is proved by works? Well, the little child will throw flowers ... I have no other means of showing my love but by throwing flowers, that is I will not let one little sacrifice escape, not one look, not one word, I will profit from all the little things and do them out of love (Ms B 196).

In this way Thérèse always retains the balance between God's action which is at work in her to will and to do the act and her own liberty, to do what she is able — and that is very little — to show her love. And Thérèse is thinking of us as she finishes her letter asking God to *choose a legion of little victims worthy of his Love* (Ms B 200).

As we come to the end of this book on Merciful Love, we could perhaps be tempted to think that, despite her weakness, Thérèse was an exceptional girl and that we are not even in the race. Then she would answer us in the form of a prayer:

I feel that if it were possible for you to find a soul weaker than mine, littler than mine, you would be pleased to grant it still greater graces, if it abandoned itself with absolute confidence to your infinite mercy.

Bibliography

Clarke, John, ocd, (translator). Saint Thérèse of Lisieux, *General Correspondence* in 2 vols. (vol. 1 1877-1890, vol. 2 1890-1897), ICS Publications, Washington DC, Vol. 1, 1982, Vol. 2, 1988.

St Thérèse of Lisieux, *Her Last Conversations*, ICS Publications, Washington DC, 1988.

Story of a Soul, The Autobiography of St Thérèse of Lisieux, ICS Publications, Washington DC, 1976.

de Meester, Conrad, *With Empty Hands*, The message of Thérèse of Lisieux, St Paul Publications, Sydney, 1982.

Geneviève of the Holy Face, Sister (Céline Martin), *A Memoir of my Sister, St Thérèse*, authorised translation of *Conseils et Souvenirs*, by the Carmelite Sisters of New York, Kennedy & Sons, New York, 1959.

John Paul II, Encyclical letter, *Dives in Misericordia*, On the Mercy of God, St Paul Publications, Sydney, 1980.

Sheed, F.J. (translator) *The Collected Letters of Saint Thérèse of Lisieux*, 1948 edition, Sheed & Ward, London, 1949.

Sion, Victor *Spiritual Realism of Saint Thérèse of Lisieux*, translated by the Carmelite Nuns, Pewaukee, Wisconsin, Bruce Publishing Co. Milwaukee, 1962.